Contents

Unit 2

READING 1

LONGMAN
KEYSTONE
A

Workbook

Anna Uhl Chamot

John De Mado

Sharroky Hollie

PEARSON
Longman

LONGMAN KEYSTONE A

Keystone A Workbook

Pearson Education, 10 Bank Street, White Plains, NY 10606

Staff credits: The people who made up the *Longman Keystone* team, representing editorial, production, design, manufacturing, and marketing, are John Ade, Rhea Banker, Liz Barker, Danielle Belfiore, Don Bensey, Virginia Bernard, Kenna Bourke, Anne Boynton-Trigg, Johnnie Farmer, Maryann Finocchi, Patrice Fraccio, Geraldine Geniusas, Charles Green, Henry Hild, David L. Jones, Lucille M. Kennedy, Ed Lamprich, Emily Lippincott, Tara Maceyak, Maria Pia Marrella, Linda Moser, Laurie Neaman, Sherri Pemberton, Liza Pleva, Joan Poole, Edie Pullman, Monica Rodriguez, Tania Saiz-Sousa, Chris Siley, Lynn Sobotta, Heather St. Clair, Jennifer Stem, Siobhan Sullivan, Jane Townsend, Heather Vomero, Marian Wassner, Lauren Weidenman, Matthew Williams, and Adina Zoltan.

Smithsonian American Art Museum contributors: Project director and writer: Elizabeth K. Eder, Ph.D.; Writer: Mary Collins; Image research assistants: Laurel Fehrenbach, Katherine G. Stilwill, and Sally Otis; Rights and reproductions: Richard H. Sorensen and Leslie G. Green; Building photograph by Tim Hursley.

Cover Image: Background, John Foxx/Getty Images; Inset, Stockbyte/Getty Images
Text composition: TSI Graphics
Text font: 11 pt ITC Stone Sans Std
Photos: 7, Dean Klevin; 11, top-right, Art Wolfe/Stone Allstock/Getty Images; 11, bottom-left, Adam Woolfitt/CORBIS; 14, 18, Andy Crawford/Dorling Kindersley; 21 Steve Vidler/SuperStock; Giorgio de Chirico, "Melancholy and Mystery of a Street," 1914. Oil on canvas, 24 1/4 × 28 1/2 in. Private Collection. Acquavella Galleries, Inc., NY. © 2008 Artists Rights Society (ARS), New York/SIAE, Rome; 39 Spencer Grant/PhotoEdit; 46, Shutterstock; 57, top (SE p116-117 bottom) bottom (SE p117 middle); 60, Jeff Greenberg/PhotoEdit. 71, Rick Whipple; 78, Bettmann/CORBIS; 85, Sunflower design and words by Lorraine Schneider, image and text® © 1968, 2003 by Another Mother for Peace, Inc (AMP) [www.anothermother. org]; 92, EyeWire Collection/Photodisc/Getty Images. 103, Sean Gallup/Getty Images; 110, Joe Sohm/Chromosohm/ Stock Connection; 117, © Ancient Art & Architecture/Danita Delimont Photography/DanitaDelimont.com; 124, Joel Sartore/National Geographic Image Collection. Peter J. Robinson/Photolibrary.com; 142, Picasso, Pablo (1881–1973)/The Bridgeman Art Library International/Hamburger Kunsthalle, Hamburg, Germany/The Bridgeman Art Library; Tom Vezo/ Nature Picture Library; 156, Dorling Kindersley; 167, Chris Lyon/Dorling Kindersley; 174, AP/Wide World Photos; 178, David A. Hardy/Photo Researchers, Inc.; 181, NASA/Finley Holiday Films/Dorling Kindersley; 188, Jose Luis Pelaez, Inc./ Bettmann/CORBIS.
Illustrations: Rick Whipple, 71
Technical art: TSI Graphics

ISBN-13: 978-0-13-241181-3
ISBN-10: 0-13-241181-4

PEARSON LONGMAN ON THE **WEB**

Pearsonlongman.com offers online resources for teachers and students. Access our Companion Websites, our online catalog, and our local offices around the world.

Visit us at **pearsonlongman.com**.

Printed in the United States of America
9 10 11–V012–12 11 10

Unit 3

READING 1

READING 2

READING 3

READING 4

Contents

Unit 4

READING 1

READING 2

READING 3

READING 4

Unit 5

READING 1

READING 2

READING 3

READING 4

Unit 6

READING 1

READING 2

READING 3

READING 4

UNIT 1 Can all mysteries be solved?

READING 1: From *Chasing Vermeer*

VOCABULARY **Literary Words** *Use with textbook page 5.*

> **REMEMBER** The people or animals in a story are called **characters**. Like real people, they have **character traits**, or qualities, that form their personalities. You learn about characters and their traits through what they say and do, and what happens to them in the story.

Decide if each phrase shows a character or character traits. Place a check mark in the correct column.

Phrase	Character	Character Trait
knows what he wants		✔
1. always looks at the bright side of things		
2. the oldest child, Paul		
3. Anansi the spider		

Read the paragraph. Then answer the questions that follow.

> Alex started packing two weeks before the camping trip. First, he asked his brother Jake if he could borrow his backpack. Jake's backpack was better for hiking than Alex's backpack. He made a list of what he needed. As he found each item, he put a check mark beside it on the list. He had everything. This was his first time camping, and he knew it was going to be perfect.

4. Who are the characters in the story?

_____

5. What character traits does Alex have?

_____

Read the paragraph below. Pay attention to the underlined academic words.

> Gravity is the force that makes things fall. It's the reason a pen falls down from a table. Isaac Newton was the first <u>individual</u> to <u>identify</u> the force of gravity. He listed several rules of gravity in 1687. He said that gravity didn't just <u>occur</u> on Earth, but also in space. His <u>theory</u> changed the way scientists saw the <u>physical</u> world.

Write the academic words from the paragraph above next to their correct definitions.

Example: _____*occur*_____: happen

1. ___theory___: an explanation that may or may not be true

2. ___physical___: relating to the body or to other things you can see, touch, smell, feel, or taste

3. ___identify___: recognize and name someone or something

4. ___individual___: a person, not a group

Use the academic words from the paragraph above to complete the sentences.

5. He wanted to be treated like an __individual__, not like one of the group.

6. I have a ___theory___ about why the woman in the painting is smiling.

7. American football is a very __physical__ game.

Complete the sentences with your own ideas.

Example: One famous theory is __the theory of gravity__.

8. I can identify _____.

9. Here is what I hope will occur this weekend: _____.

10. My favorite physical activity is _____.

WORD STUDY Prefixes *un-, dis-* Use with textbook page 7.

REMEMBER A prefix is a word part added to the beginning of a word that changes the word's meaning. Some prefixes have more than one meaning. For example, the prefix *un-* means "not" or "the opposite of." The prefix *dis-* means "not," "outside of," or "the opposite of." Knowing the meanings of prefixes can help you figure out the meanings of many words you read and hear.

Look at the chart below. Add the prefixes *un-* or *dis-* to each base word to create a new word. Write the new word on the chart. Then write the meaning of the new word.

Prefix	Word	New Word	Definition
un-	wrap	*unwrap*	*"not wrapped"*
1. un-	clear		
2. un-	qualified		
3. dis-	satisfied		
4. dis-	pleased		
5. dis-	content		

Create a new word by adding the prefix *un-* or *dis-* to each word below. Check a dictionary if necessary. Then write the definition next to the new word.

Example: pleasant _____*unpleasant* "not pleasant"_____

6. honest _____

7. organized _____

8. finished _____

9. necessary _____

10. afraid _____

REMEMBER You can look for clues in a story that help you predict what will happen next.

Read the paragraphs and answer the questions that follow.

> If he could just strike out one more player, Christopher's team would win the game. He held the softball in his hand as the next batter stepped up. The batter looked at Christopher and then up and over his head. Christopher turned to see what he was looking at. The big gray cloud was just about to cover the sun. If it started to rain, the game would be postponed. Christopher didn't want that to happen.
>
> He threw a pitch. The batter swung and hit a foul ball. One strike. Just two more, thought Christopher. The whole field was dark now because of the cloud. He threw the ball. Just one more strike, thought Christopher. But in the distance, he heard a rumble of thunder.

1. What is happening at the beginning of this story?

   _____

2. What is Christopher trying to do?

   _____

3. What may prevent Christopher from doing what he wants?

   _____

4. Make a prediction about what will happen next.

   _____

5. How can the skill of making a prediction help you to become a better reader?

   _____

   _____

COMPREHENSION *Use with textbook page 14.*

Choose the best answer for each item. Circle the letter of the correct answer.

1. Students thought Ms. Hussey _____.

   a. was quiet and   **b.** was excited   **c.** was bored with
       unhappy   about learning   her job

2. In the first weeks of school, the class studied _____.

   a. a lot of different things   **b.** their textbook   **c.** one subject

3. The book Petra found listed hundreds of _____.

   a. events in the future   **b.** historical events   **c.** strange events

4. Ms. Hussey's class discussed the best way to _____.

   a. write   **b.** communicate   **c.** read

5. The book Petra found was special to her because _____.

   a. it was full of quotes   **b.** it had lots of   **c.** it encouraged people
      from newspapers   illustrations   to study unknown things

RESPONSE TO LITERATURE *Use with textbook page 15.*

The book Petra found told about strange events. Choose one of the strange events. Use details to write a paragraph describing it.

_____

_____

_____

_____

_____

GRAMMAR, USAGE, AND MECHANICS

Distinguishing Parts of Speech *Use with textbook page 16.*

REMEMBER A sentence always contains a subject and a verb. It may also contain an object. A subject (a noun, pronoun, or noun phrase) performs the action. A verb describes an action, a fact, or a state. An object (also a noun, pronoun, or noun phrase) receives the action. **Example:** I drove the car. Objects may follow a preposition. A preposition (such as *at, on, in, above, behind,* or *before*) may show location and time. **Example:** I drove the car to the shop.

Complete the chart with words from the box. Write each word under its part of speech.

draws	in	before	real	house	new	Picasso	he	rice	loves

Noun or Pronoun		Adjective	Verb	Preposition

Form sentences with the words and phrases in parentheses. Put the parts of speech in the correct order.

Example: (see / the children / at the zoo / animals)

The children see animals at the zoo.

1. (play / the children)

_____

2. (play/ at school / the children)

_____

3. (children / the friendly / play / at school)

_____

4. (children / the friendly / at school / with each other / play)

_____

5. (in the morning / the children / at school / with each other / play)

_____

WRITING A DESCRIPTIVE PARAGRAPH

Describe a Character *Use with textbook page 17.*

This is the T-chart that Andrew completed before writing his paragraph.

Physical traits	Character traits
long ponytail three earrings in each ear	fascinating honest unpredictable excited listens carefully

Complete your own T-chart for a paragraph describing Petra.

Physical traits	Character traits

Can all mysteries be solved?

READING 2: From *G Is for Googol*

VOCABULARY **Key Words** *Use with textbook page 19.*

Write each word in the box next to its definition.

architecture	gradual	infinity	numerals	spirals	steep

Example: _architecture_ : the style and design of buildings

1. _____: happening or changing slowly over a long time

2. _____: rising or falling sharply

3. _____: written signs that represent numbers

4. _____: shapes that curve around and around as they go up

5. _____: space or distance that has no limits or end

Use the words in the box at the top of the page to complete the sentences.

6. Long ago, people in Europe used Roman _____ to write numbers.

7. There was a slow, _____ change in the temperature from hot to cold.

8. In modern _____, buildings are often made of concrete, steel, and glass.

9. The path was level at first, but it grew _____ as we climbed the hill.

10. Many flowers grow in _____, curving out from the center.

VOCABULARY **Academic Words** *Use with textbook page 20.*

Read the paragraph below. Pay attention to the underlined academic words.

I found a very <u>unique</u> book in the library. It's a book on how to grow carnivorous plants—plants that eat insects. The book uses photographs to <u>illustrate</u> the <u>sequence</u> of steps you need to follow to grow and care for the plants. And because you'll need a <u>constant</u> supply of insects for your plants, the book also tells how to attract and catch flies!

Write the letter of the correct definition next to each word.

Example: ___*b*___ constant

_____ **1.** illustrate

_____ **2.** sequence

_____ **3.** unique

a. the only one of its type

b. happening regularly or all the time

c. explain or make something clear by giving examples

d. a series of related events, actions, or numbers that have a particular order

Use the academic words from the exercise above to complete the sentences.

4. My teacher will _____ an event in history by describing other events like it.

5. Every person has a _____ fingerprint.

6. The _____ noise in the city gave me a headache.

7. Do you remember the _____ of events in the story?

Complete the sentences with your own ideas.

Example: Every snowflake has a unique _____*pattern*_____.

8. It is good to drive at a constant _____.

9. I like to illustrate my ideas by _____.

10. There is a particular sequence of steps to _____.

WORD STUDY Spelling Words with *ai, ay, ee,* and *oa*

Use with textbook page 21.

> **REMEMBER** Vowel digraphs, or vowel teams, are two letters that work as a team to stand for one vowel sound. For example in the word *goat*, the digraph *oa* stands for one sound: the /ō/ sound. The digraphs *ai, ay, ee,* or *oa* often stand for a long vowel sound, usually the sound of the first letter. Remember this rhyme: "When two vowels go walking, the first one does the talking." For example, the digraph *ai* in *mail* stands for /ā/.

Read the words in the box below quietly to yourself. Listen for the long vowel sound. Then sort the words according to the long vowel sound and its spelling. Write each word in the correct column in the chart.

~~sail~~	straight	coast	disagree	Wednesday	roast
raise	goat	bleed	portray	queen	delay

/ā/ spelled ai	/ā/ spelled ay	/ē/ spelled ee	/ō/ spelled oa
sail			

Circle the vowel digraph that stands for a long vowel sound in each word below. Then use each word in a sentence of your own.

Example: r(oa)d _We drove down a long and bumpy dirt road._

1. paycheck _____

2. steel _____

3. afraid _____

4. toad _____

5 stain _____

6. yesterday _____

7. weekend _____

8. wait _____

9. boast _____

Name _____ Date _____

> **REMEMBER** Visuals are the pictures, charts, graphs, maps, and diagrams that can come with a text. You can use visuals in a text to learn more about the topic.

Look at the pictures, chart, and text. Answer the questions that follow.

The Mysteries of Stonehenge and Easter Island

Mysterious Statues

Easter Island is a small island, thousands of miles off the coast of Chile. When explorers reached the island, they found almost 900 statues of figures. Researchers believe that these may have been statues of gods.

Distance that the stones were carried

Monument	Distance
Stonehenge	480 km/300 miles
Easter Island	23 km/14 miles

A Puzzling Monument

Stonehenge in England is a series of big stones arranged in a circle. The monument was built 5,000 years ago, and some believe it was created to measure the sun's movement. But without information from the people who built it, no one can be sure.

1. Underline the title and circle the headings. What do you think the article will be about?

   _____

2. Draw an *x* over any pictures. How does the picture help you to understand the text?

   _____

3. Circle the table. How does the table help you to understand the text?

   _____

4. In one sentence, summarize the article.

   _____

5. How do you think using visuals can help you to understand a text?

   _____

Choose the best answer for each item. Circle the letter of the correct answer.

1. You find the next number in the Fibonacci sequence by _____.

   a. adding the previous two   **b.** subtracting the previous two   **c.** dividing the last one by two

2. Because of Fibonacci, we now use _____.

   a. Italian numerals   **b.** Roman numerals   **c.** Arabic numerals

3. The bracts, or knobby parts, of pinecones grow in _____.

   a. straight lines   **b.** squares   **c.** spirals

4. The Fibonacci sequence is a special _____.

   a. way to do things   **b.** number pattern   **c.** type of plant

5. Fibonacci numbers are often found in _____.

   a. nature   **b.** water   **c.** the air

EXTENSION *Use with textbook page 27.*

Draw a picture of a new plant or flower. Imagine that you discovered it in the wild, so you must name it. As you draw it, make sure it has patterns. It may have a certain number of blooms or leaves or a certain number of designs in it. Label the patterns.

Name _____ Date _____

Making Comparisons: *-er than* and *as . . . as* Use with textbook page 28.

REMEMBER Comparative adjectives compare two things. To form the comparative of a one-syllable adjective, add *-r* or *-er*. **Example:** This mystery book is *stranger* than the last one.
With some adjectives, the last letter is doubled before *-er* is added. **Example:** My cousin's pet pig is *fatter* than mine.
To form the comparative of an adjective ending in *-y*, change the *y* to *i* and add *-er*. **Example:** The sequel is sillier than the first film.
Usually, *than* follows a comparative adjective. *As . . . as* shows that two things are equal. *Not as . . . as* shows that two things are unequal.
Examples: She is just *as smart as* he is. Sally is not as good a soccer player as Katja.

Complete each sentence below with an adjective from the box.

hotter	foamy	deeper	younger	fast

1. I can run as __fast__ as my brother.

2. The water at this end of the pool is __deeper__ than the water at the other end.

3. Today it is two degrees __hotter__ in Florida than in Kansas.

4. During a storm, the waves are as __foamy__ as root beer.

5. The sixth-graders are __younger__ than the seventh-graders.

Complete each sentence below with the correct form of the adjective in parentheses. You may not need to change its form.

Example: (lazy) The cat is __lazier__ than the dog.

6. (soapy) The water in the sink is __soapier__ than the water in the tub.

7. (sad) The clown looks __sadder__ than the magician.

8. (steep) The cliff is almost as __steep__ as a wall.

9. (narrow) This road is not as __narrow__ as it was before the construction project.

10. (soft) The fabric feels as __soft__ as silk.

Describe an Object *Use with textbook page 29.*

This is the word web that Wendy completed before writing her paragraph.

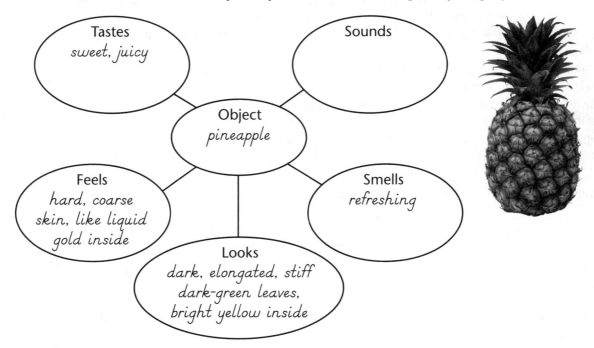

Tastes
sweet, juicy

Sounds

Object
pineapple

Feels
*hard, coarse
skin, like liquid
gold inside*

Smells
refreshing

Looks
*dark, elongated, stiff
dark-green leaves,
bright yellow inside*

Complete your own word web for a paragraph describing a fruit or vegetable. Include sensory details.

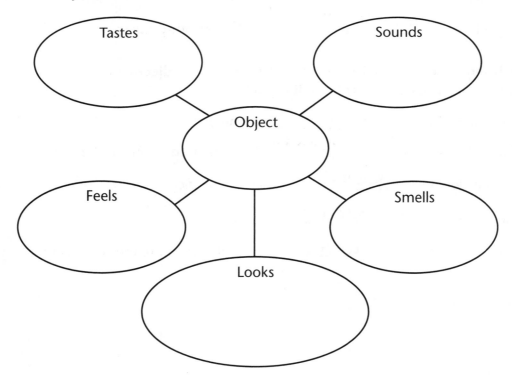

Tastes

Sounds

Object

Feels

Smells

Looks

Can all mysteries be solved?

READING 3: "Fact or Fiction?"

VOCABULARY **Key Words** *Use with textbook page 31.*

Write each word in the box next to its definition.

archaeologist	clues	creature	disappeared	fantasy	sacred

Example: _____*sacred*_____: relating to a god or religion and believed to be holy

1. ___*creature*___: an animal, fish, or insect

2. ___*archaeologist*___: someone who learns about ancient civilizations by studying the remains of their graves, buildings, and tools

3. ___*disappeared*___: stopped existing

4. ___*clues*___: information or objects that can help solve a crime or mystery

5. ___*fantasy*___: a thing or a situation that is not real, but imagined

Use the words in the box at the top of the page to complete the sentences.

6. A detective looks for ___*clues*___ to solve a mystery.

7. The starfish is a ___*creature*___ that lives in water.

8. Scientists are still trying to decide why the dinosaurs ___*disappeared*___.

9. Another word for holy is ___*sacred*___.

10. I have a dream about becoming a star, but it is just a ___*fantasy*___.

Read the paragraph below. Pay attention to the underlined academic words.

Why did the dinosaurs disappear? A recent theory is that dinosaurs were killed when an asteroid hit Earth. An asteroid could <u>create</u> enough dust to block out the sun for a long time, killing the plants on Earth. The dinosaurs would not have had enough food to <u>survive</u>. The asteroid theory is supported by new <u>evidence</u>. Many scientists believe this is the most <u>accurate</u> theory on the disappearance of the dinosaurs.

Write the academic words from the paragraph above next to their correct definitions.

Example: _____*survive*_____: continue to live or exist

1. ____*evidence*____: facts, objects, or signs that make you believe that something exists or is true

2. ____*create*____: make something exist

3. ____*accurate*____: correct or exact

Use the academic words from the paragraph above to complete the sentences.

4. You can use computer programs to ____*create*____ drawings on the screen.

5. My watch is very ____*accurate*____.

6. Some animals can ____*survive*____ for a long time without food.

7. Right now, we have no ____*evidence*____ that there is life on other planets.

Complete the sentences with your own ideas.

Example: The pyramids are evidence that the people of Egypt
____*knew how to build huge buildings*____.

8. If my research is not accurate, my paper will _____.

9. To survive in a cold climate, I would have to _____.

10. I want to create a new _____.

WORD STUDY Same Sound, Different Spellings

Use with textbook page 33.

> **REMEMBER** The sound /ər/ can be spelled different ways when it comes at the end of a word in an unstressed syllable. It can be spelled *ar* as in *dollar*, *er* as in *pitcher*, or *or* as in *actor*.

Read the words in the box below. Then write each word in the correct column in the chart.

nectar	tractor	cracker	doctor	collar
silver	winter	color	beggar	

/ər/ spelled ar	/ər/ spelled er	/ər/ spelled or
nectar		

Write the letters that stand for the /ər/ sound in each word below. Then use each word in a sentence of your own. Use a dictionary if you are unsure of a word's meaning.

Example: cedar ___ar___ *We have a cedar tree in our backyard.* _____

1. particular _____

2. motor _____

3. splinter _____

4. finger _____

5. summer _____

6. splendor _____

7. scholar _____

REMEMBER You can preview the pictures and headings in a passage to prepare yourself for the information you are about to learn.

Look at the picture, headings, and text. Answer the questions that follow.

A Rainbow of Colors

Try Fruits of Different Colors

You probably know that fruits come in a range of colors. But did you know that different colored fruits provide different nutrients? Nutritionists recommend eating fruit from as many different colors as you can each day.

Red, Green, Blue, and White Fruit

Red fruits include raspberries, red grapes, and watermelon. Greens include green grapes and kiwi fruit. Blueberries are a blue fruit and white peaches are a white fruit.

Fruits come in many colors, and eating a variety of colored fruits is good for you.

1. Circle the title and underline the headings. What do you think the article is about?

   _____

2. Turn each heading into a question.

   _____

   _____

3. Look at the picture and its caption. What does it tell you about the article?

   _____

4. Set a purpose for reading the article.

   _____

5. How can the skill of previewing help you to understand a text?

   _____

   _____

COMPREHENSION   *Use with textbook page 40.*

Choose the best answer for each item. Circle the letter of the correct answer.

1. The buildings of Machu Picchu were made of _____.

   a. cement   **b.** wood   **c.** stone blocks

2. Some people think Stonehenge was built as a huge _____.

   a. calendar   **b.** thermometer   **c.** ruler

3. Many creatures underwater _____.

   a. are imaginary   **b.** remain a mystery   **c.** are as big as the
                                         to humans   Loch Ness monster

4. Some people think the Loch Ness monster is _____.

   a. a truck   **b.** a sheep   **c.** a fantasy

5. The creature Bigfoot _____.

   a. has supposedly been spotted   **b.** is half human,   **c.** has been proven
       in more than one country   half bear   to be a fake

EXTENSION   *Use with textbook page 41.*

What was a favorite creature of yours when you were young? Was it real or imaginary? If it was imaginary, did it look like any real creatures? Write the name of the creature at the top of the chart. Find or invent information about it. Use the information to complete the rest of the chart.

Name	
Location	
Description	
Behavior	

GRAMMAR, USAGE, AND MECHANICS

Passive Voice *Use with textbook page 42.*

REMEMBER A verb in the active voice tells who or what performs the action.
Example: I walk to school every day.
A verb in the passive voice tells who or what receives the action. Form the passive voice with a form of
be + a past participle. A *by*-phrase identifies the performer.
Example: The famous monument *was passed* by all the tourists.

**Read each sentence. Write *active* on the line if the sentence is in the active voice.
Write *passive* if the sentence is in the passive voice.**

Example: _____*active*_____ The Inca left Machu Picchu in the early 1550s.

1. _____ Orion's Belt was considered sacred by the Egyptians.

2. _____ Hiram Bingham explored Machu Picchu in 1911.

3. _____ Heavy stones were moved 14 miles by the Rapa Nui.

4. _____ British archaeologists opened Tutankhamen's tomb in 1922.

5. _____ A sea monster was seen by a man from Norway.

Rewrite each sentence by writing the verb in the passive voice.

Example: Archaeologists find treasures.

_____*Treasures are found by archaeologists.*_____

6. An engineer noticed the shape of the pyramids.

_____

7. The Great Sphinx defends the pyramids.

_____

8. Wind and sand eroded the sculpture.

_____

9. No one understands the Rapa Nui language.

_____

10. Perhaps the stones measured solstices.

_____

WRITING a DESCRIPTIVE PARAGRAPH

Describe a Place *Use with textbook page 43.*

This is the pyramid that Angelina completed before writing her paragraph.

Top *spectacular view*
Middle *ninety-one steps*
Bottom *inner temple, statue of jaguar*

Complete your own pyramid for a paragraph that describes a mysterious place.

Top
Middle
Bottom

Can all mysteries be solved?

READING 4: "Teenage Detectives"

VOCABULARY **Literary Words** *Use with textbook page 45.*

> **REMEMBER** **Idioms** are expressions that have a different meaning from the words that make them up.
> **Example:** *Under the weather* means "not feeling well." **Puns** are jokes that use a word with more than one meaning, or words that sound the same but have different meanings.
> **Example:** The magician was so angry he pulled his hare out. (*Hare* is an animal similar to a rabbit. *Hare* sounds like the *hair* that grows on your head.)

The sentences below use either puns or idioms. Put a check mark in the correct column for each one.

Sentence	Pun	Idiom
The dress was very expensive; it cost an arm and a leg.		✔
1. One of these new shoes isn't right.		
2. The show was so funny I nearly split my sides laughing.		
3. At first, I couldn't figure out how to fasten my seatbelt, but then it clicked.		
4. Josh spilled the beans about the surprise party.		
5. She has a real green thumb; plants always grow for her.		

Many idioms include references to animals. Some animal idioms are shown in the web below. Think of at least five more idioms that refer to animals. Write them in the circles. If you can think of more idioms, add more circles.

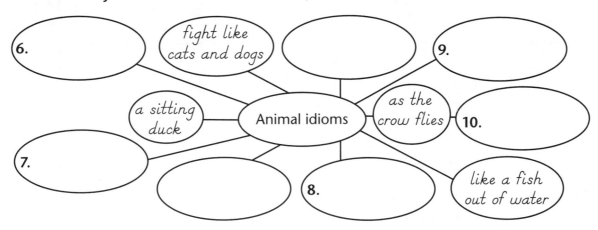

VOCABULARY   Academic Words *Use with textbook page 46.*

Read the paragraph below. Pay attention to the underlined academic words.

Mysteries are popular because readers like to feel like they are crime solvers. In a mystery novel, a detective tries to solve a crime and <u>pursue</u> a criminal. To do this he must look for clues, and also figure out the <u>motive</u> behind the crime. The criminal is usually very <u>intelligent</u> and makes this difficult. The most exciting part of the story is when the reader becomes <u>aware</u> of all the clues and tries to figure out who the criminal is.

Write the letter of the correct definition next to each word.

Example: ___c___ motive

_____ **1.** pursue

_____ **2.** aware

_____ **3.** intelligent

a. chase or follow someone or something to catch him, her, or it

b. having a high ability to learn, understand, and think about things

c. the reason that makes someone do something, especially when this reason is kept hidden

d. realizing that something is true, exists, or is happening

Use the academic words from the exercise above to complete the sentences.

4. My dog is so _____; I think he understands everything I say!

5. Detectives try to find out who had a _____ to commit a crime.

6. Some detectives put on a disguise to _____ a criminal without being seen.

7. Since it was getting dark, the hikers were not _____ that there was a fallen tree lying in the path.

Complete the sentences with your own ideas.

Example: The scientist's motive for doing research was ___*to find a cure*___.

8. I wonder if there is intelligent life _____.

9. I am aware that _____.

10. A career I want to pursue is _____.

> **REMEMBER** A compound noun is made up of two or more words. Compound nouns can be written as one word, as in *eyelash*. They can be written as two separate words, as in *web page*. They can be written with a hyphen, as in *father-in-law*. Check the compound noun in a dictionary if you are not sure how to spell it.

Combine the words from the first two columns to form compound nouns. Use a dictionary to find out whether the words are written as one word, as two words, or with a hyphen.

Word 1	Word 2	Compound Noun
book	keeper	*bookkeeper*
air	conditioner	*air conditioner*
great	grandfather	*great-grandfather*
1. light	house	
2. butter	milk	
3. ice	skater	
4. barn	yard	
5. brother	in-law	

Create compound nouns by adding a word from the box to the beginning of each word below. Check your work in a dictionary to see if the compound noun is written as one word, as two words, or with a hyphen.

~~key~~	fire	sea	merry	shoe	apple

Example: _____*key*_____ board

6. _____ -go-round

7. _____ sauce

8. _____ lace

9. _____ shell

10. _____ drill

READING STRATEGY | DRAW CONCLUSIONS   *Use with textbook page 47.*

REMEMBER To draw conclusions about a text, use clues from the text and your own experience and knowledge to figure out what the author means.

Read the paragraph and answer the questions that follow.

Ella Olensky had just arrived in the Los Angeles airport. America! She couldn't believe she was finally here. As she handed her Russian passport to the officer, she could not help but smile.

1. Where is Ella Olensky from?

   _____

2. What clues from the text and/or knowledge from your own experience helped you to draw a conclusion about where she is from?

   _____

   _____

3. How does Ella Olensky feel about arriving in Los Angeles?

   _____

   _____

4. What clues from the text and/or knowledge from your own experience helped you to draw a conclusion about how she feels about arriving in Los Angeles?

   _____

   _____

5. How can the skill of drawing conclusions help you to become a better reader?

   _____

   _____

Choose the best answer for each item. Circle the letter of the correct answer.

1. In "The Case of the Defaced Sidewalk," Nina found out who _____.

   a. jumped in wet concrete   **b.** had wide feet   **c.** needed new shoes

2. Max's mom wants to know what happened at the house because _____.

   a. she knows who lives there   **b.** she used to live there   **c.** she is the real estate agent

3. The missing signs in "The Case of the Disappearing Signs" were _____.

   a. FOR SALE signs   **b.** street signs   **c.** stop signs

4. The biggest clue in "The Case of the Disappearing Signs" was _____.

   a. a pickup truck   **b.** a fire in July   **c.** a lawnmower

5. To figure things out, Max and Nina look for _____.

   a. a magnifying glass   **b.** clues   **c.** fireplaces

RESPONSE TO LITERATURE *Use with textbook page 55.*

Find a paragraph that you like very much in the story. Draw a picture illustrating the images the paragraph presents. Write in dialogue for the people in the picture.

GRAMMAR, USAGE, AND MECHANICS

Subject-Verb Agreement with Indefinite Pronouns *Use with textbook page 56.*

REMEMBER An indefinite pronoun names a person, place, or thing that is not specific. They are used to make generalizations or to refer to a previously used noun.
Example: Why would *someone* go to Iceland?
If the indefinite pronoun is the subject of the sentence, the verb agrees and becomes singular or plural according to the indefinite pronoun.
Example: *Everyone* was at the party.

Circle the verb in each sentence that agrees with the indefinite pronoun.

Example: Something ((is)/ are) wrong.

1. Almost everyone (know / knows) his name.

2. Few of them (notice / notices) her new hairstyle.

3. Someone (park / parks) his or her car there every morning.

4. Many (was / were) curious.

5. Each (give / gives) her own version of the story.

Write sentences with the indefinite pronoun and verb in parentheses. If necessary, change the form of the verb so that it agrees with the pronoun.

Example: (nobody + like) *Nobody in our house likes spinach.*

6. (everybody + say)

_____

7. (someone + drive)

_____

8. (many + stare)

_____

9. (nothing + happen)

_____

10. (few + ask)

_____

WRITING A DESCRIPTIVE PARAGRAPH

Describe an Event *Use with textbook page 57.*

This is the sequence chart that Anna completed before writing her paragraph.

First *I hid the hula hoop in a shopping bag under a pile of clothes in the closet*

↓

Next *Mom asked Sue to take some old clothes to our local thrift shop.*

↓

Then *I had a chance to wrap the gift, but the hoop had vanished.*

↓

Finally *a week later, I figured out what happened.*

Complete your own sequence chart for a paragraph about a made-up event.

↓

↓

↓

↓

EDIT AND PROOFREAD   *Use with textbook page 64.*

Read the paragraph below carefully. Look for mistakes in spelling, punctuation, and grammar. Mark the mistakes with proofreader's marks (textbook page 454). Then rewrite the paragraph correctly on the lines below.

This summer a new family moved next door to us. I hoped their would be kids my age, but they just have a new baby She's cute, but I'm not really interested in babysiting. They have a dog, though, wich is a lot of fun. He is a retriever, and his name is toby. He's still prety young. He likes to be walk a lot Because of the baby, Toby sometimes doesn't get enough attention. when I get home from school, I ask if I can take him for a walk. We go to the park and I threw his tennis ball for him. Toby loves that game. I throw the ball until my arm gets tired. Then we run back home together. we both have a lot of fun.

_____

_____

_____

_____

_____

_____

_____

_____

_____

_____

_____

Underline the vocabulary items you know and can use well. Review and practice any you haven't underlined. Underline them when you know them well.

Literary Words	Key Words	Academic Words	
characters	architecture	identify	accurate
character traits	gradual	individual	create
idioms	infinity	occur	evidence
puns	numerals	physical	survive
	spirals	theory	aware
	steep	constant	intelligent
	archaeologist	illustrate	motive
	clues	sequence	pursue
	creature	unique	
	disappeared		
	fantasy		
	sacred		

Put a check by the skills you can perform well. Review and practice any you haven't checked off. Check them off when you can perform them well.

Skills	I can . . .
Word Study	☐ recognize and use the prefixes *un-, dis-*. ☐ spell words with *ai, ay, ee,* and *oa*. ☐ spell words with the same sound but different spellings. ☐ recognize and use compound nouns.
Reading Strategies	☐ predict. ☐ use visuals. ☐ preview. ☐ draw conclusions.
Grammar, Usage, and Mechanics	☐ distinguish parts of speech. ☐ make comparisons with *-er than* and *as…as*. ☐ use the passive voice. ☐ use correct subject-verb agreement with indefinite pronouns.
Writing	☐ describe a character. ☐ describe an object. ☐ describe a place. ☐ describe an event. ☐ write a descriptive essay.

Learn about Art with the Smithsonian American Art Museum *Use with textbook pages 66–67*

LEARNING TO LOOK

Look at *Preamble* by Mike Wilkins on page 66. Describe six things you see in this artwork. State facts, not opinions.

Example: *Many of the license plates are blue.*

1. _____

2. _____

3. _____

4. _____

5. _____

6. _____

INTERPRETATION

Look at *Five* by Robert Indiana on page 67. Imagine that you are driving down the highway and see *Five* on the side of the road. What do you see? Write where you think the artwork is telling you to go.

Example: *It's a sign for an old general store and it's telling me it's just five miles ahead.*

_____

_____

_____

_____

_____

_____

_____

Look at *Preamble* by Mike Wilkins on page 66. Imagine you could interview the artist about this artwork. What would you want to know? Use *Who, Where, When, What, Why,* and *How* to frame your questions.

Example: How *did you get the idea for this artwork?*

1. Who _____

_____

2. Where _____

_____

3. When _____

_____

4. What _____

_____

5. Why _____

_____

6. How _____

_____

Name _____ Date _____

UNIT 2

How does growing up change us?

READING 1: "Ancient Kids"

VOCABULARY **Key Words** *Use with textbook page 71.*

Write each word in the box next to its definition.

ancient	ceremony	citizen	education	rights	rituals

Example: ____*rights*____: things you are allowed to do, according to law or moral ideas

1. _____: process of learning in a school or other program of study

2. _____: ceremonies that are always done the same way

3. _____: someone who lives in a particular town, state, or country

4. _____: formal event that happens in public on special occasions

5. _____: happening or existing very far back in history

Use the words in the box at the top of the page to complete the sentences.

6. My grandfather is a _____ of the United States of America.

7. I believe that every child should go to school and get a good _____.

8. The mask the archaeologist found in the old palace was _____.

9. The priest performed all of the _____ the same way every week.

10. A family member's wedding _____ is a very important tradition in my family.

Read the paragraph below. Pay attention to the underlined academic words.

The arts and literature of the <u>classical</u> societies of Greece and Rome still have an impact on our own <u>cultural</u> life today. Each <u>feature</u> of ancient art can be seen in the paintings and sculptures of our own day and time. The writings of Greek philosophers, such as Plato and Socrates, still influence modern <u>philosophy</u>. And modern plays have many elements from classical theater.

Write the academic words from the paragraph above next to their correct definitions.

Example: ___*philosophy*___ : the study of what it means to exist, what good and evil are, what knowledge is, or how people should live

1. _____ : quality, element, or characteristic of something that seems important, interesting, or typical

2. _____ : relating to a particular society and its way of life

3. _____ : belonging to the culture of ancient Greece or ancient Rome

Use the academic words from the paragraph above to complete the sentences.

4. An interesting _____ of this flower is its unusual petals.

5. I want to study the _____ writers of the Roman period in my English class.

6. Studying _____ made her wonder about the meaning of life.

7. There are many _____ differences between the two countries.

Complete the sentences with your own ideas.

Example: I think that life in classical Greece was ___*very exciting*___ .

8. One feature I have that is unusual is _____ .

9. I think that attending cultural activities and sporting events is _____

_____ .

10. The study of philosophy is _____ .

WORD STUDY Spelling Words with Long Vowel Sound /ē/

Use with textbook page 73.

> **REMEMBER** The long /ē/ sound can be spelled several different ways. These include *e* as in *she*, *ee* as in *street*, *ea* as in *wheat*, *ie* as in *yield*, *y* as in *lady*, and *ey* as in *donkey*. Knowing these patterns helps you spell and say the words correctly.

Read the words in the box. Then write each word in the correct column in the chart.

even	each	irony	achieve	monkey	thief
season	shady	evil	beet	attorney	weekend

Long e spelled *e*	Long e spelled *ee*	Long e spelled *ea*
even	weekend	each
evil	beet	season

Long e spelled *ie*	Long e spelled *y*	Long e spelled *ey*
achieve	irony	monkey
thief	shady	attorney

Write the letter-sound pattern in each word.

Example: we   *long /e/ spelled e*

1. cheap   _____

2. chief   _____

3. botany   _____

4. barley   _____

5. speed   _____

6. agony   _____

7. sweet   _____

8. siege   _____

9. speak   _____

Use with textbook page 73.

REMEMBER Comparing and contrasting things in a selection help you recall what you read. When you compare, you show how things, ideas, facts, persons, events, and stories are the same. When you contrast, you show how things, ideas, facts, persons, events, and stories are different.

Read each paragraph and answer the questions that follow.

Connor missed his friends and his room at home in the city. He wanted to play soccer down at the park and go for ice cream afterwards. He even missed the school and the cars buzzing by the playground all afternoon.

After a while, however, he began to like it at his grandfather's house. The quiet was so different from home. And he loved the bay. He liked fishing and throwing stones into the water. He even liked hearing about his grandfather's time in the military.

1. How are the city and the bay different?

   _____

2. How does Connor feel about the different places he has lived?

   _____

Sarah was puzzled. She looked at the two dogs. They were so different. One was small and fluffy and jumped around a lot. The other was bigger, moved less, and gave Sarah goofy looks.

The man who ran the shelter said, "They are both two years old and ready for adoption. It really depends on what you're looking for."

Sarah thought she was looking for a small dog. However, there was something about the big eyes of the bigger dog she really liked. This was going to be a tough decision.

3. In what ways are the dogs alike?

   _____

4. In what ways are the dogs different?

   _____

5. How does comparing and contrasting help you to understand a story?

   _____

COMPREHENSION   *Use with textbook page 80.*

Choose the best answer for each item. Circle the letter of the correct answer.

1. In ancient Greece, boys went to school and _____.

    a. girls went to school, too   **b.** girls stayed at home and helped their mothers   **c.** girls worked outside of the home

2. What did boys in ancient Greece learn about at school?

    a. the arts, war, and how to be a good citizen   **b.** science, technology, and computers   **c.** English, Spanish, and Chinese

3. Who was the "head of the family" in ancient Rome?

    a. the eldest son in the family   **b.** the mother   **c.** the oldest male in the family

4. Which jobs were women in ancient Rome not allowed to have?

    a. lawyer, teacher, and government jobs   **b.** mother and homemaker   **c.** farmer and maker of crafts

5. Did poor children go to school in ancient Rome?

    a. Yes, they went to school.   **b.** No, they studied at home with their parents.   **c.** They did not go to school or study anywhere.

EXTENSION   *Use with textbook page 81.*

In the column on the left, list five things that you think were fun about living in one of the ancient cultures you read about. In the column on the right, list five things that you think were difficult about living in one of the ancient cultures.

Fun Times	Difficult Times
learning how to sail boats	*girls couldn't continue in school*

GRAMMAR, USAGE, AND MECHANICS

Showing Contrast: Transitions and Coordinating Conjunctions

Use with textbook page 82.

> **REMEMBER** Certain transitions and coordinating conjunctions show differences between two things. The transitions *however* and *on the other hand* and the coordinating conjunctions *but* and *yet* show differences. Use a comma after *however* and *on the other hand* and before *but* or *yet*.
> **Examples:** My family wants to go skiing. However, it didn't snow very much this month. My friend loves reading books, but I prefer watching movies.

Choose a phrase or sentence from the boxes to make a sentence or sentences that will make the best contrast.

but they did have a system of writing.	On the other hand, they also offer great enjoyment.	However, Romans used bricks.	yet they also grew cotton and beans.	~~but the Greeks built things of great beauty~~.

Example: The Romans built useful things.

The Romans built useful things, but the Greeks built things of great beauty.

1. Greeks used marble in their buildings.

   _____

2. The Maya people's main crop was corn.

   _____

Write a new sentence that will contrast with each sentence. Follow the instructions in parentheses.

Example: (Use *However.*) Both cats and dogs make good pets.

However, only cats catch mice.

3. (Use *On the other hand.*) Sometimes rainy days are boring.

   _____

4. (Use *But.*) Spinach is good for you.

   _____.

5. (Use *However.*) Both gold and silver are metals.

   _____

WRITING A NARRATIVE PARAGRAPH

Write a Friendly Letter *Use with textbook page 83.*

This is the "parts of a letter" organizer that Tyler completed before writing his letter.

> (Date)
> *July 23, 2009*
>
> (Greeting)
> *Dear Grandpa,*
>
> (Body)
> *Did I ever tell you how being in my school play helped me overcome stage fright?*
> *I didn't really enjoy performing in front of others. I was nervous.*
> *I performed well. I felt an amazing sense of accomplishment.*
>
> (Closing) *Love,*
> (Signature) *Tyler*

Complete your own "parts of a letter" organizer for a friendly letter to an older family member.

> (Date)
>
> (Greeting)
>
> (Body)
>
>
>
>
>
>
> (Closing)
> (Signature)

How does growing up change us?

READING 2: From *Becoming Naomi León*

VOCABULARY **Literary Words** *Use with textbook page 85.*

REMEMBER **Dialogue** is the exact words spoken by two or more characters. Writers use dialogue to show what the characters in a story are like.
Example: "I am too tired to play another game," said Rosa.
The **setting** is the time and place where a story occurs. Identifying the setting will help you understand what is happening in the story.
Example: The sun rose so hot over the Arizona desert that Lucia awoke at first light.

Read each sentence. Write *setting* if it describes a setting. Write *dialogue* if it gives words spoken by characters.

Setting or Dialogue	Sentence
setting	When I was a young man, I lived in New York City. It was 1920, the year I turned fifteen.
1.	Julie pressed her face to the airplane window. "Oh Mom, I'm so excited!" she said. "In another hour we'll be in France!"
2.	Nate woke up and immediately remembered that it was New Year's Day. "Welcome to 2008," he said to himself.
3.	Mandy had lived in the same small town in Ohio her whole life. She loved it there. She had known all her friends since kindergarten.
4.	I'd never really wanted to visit my aunt in Mexico, but now that I was spending the summer here, I was very excited.
5.	It was the year 1988. I'd just started the sixth grade at Bedford Junior High in Marion, Kentucky.

On the lines below write a brief dialogue. You can use made-up characters or people you know. Be sure to give a setting.

_____

_____

_____

_____

VOCABULARY   Academic Words   *Use with textbook page 86.*

Read the paragraph. Pay attention to the underlined academic words.

> Sometimes two people have a <u>conflict</u> they can't solve. In this case, it's often wise to seek a counselor. The counselor can <u>assist</u> by guiding them through the <u>process</u> of conflict resolution. The counselor can also help them strengthen the <u>bond</u> they feel with each other.

Write the letter of the correct definition next to each word.

Example: ___*c*___ assist

_____ 1. conflict

_____ 2. bond

_____ 3. process

a. a series of actions that someone does in order to achieve a particular result

b. disagreement

c. help someone do something

d. a feeling or interest that unites two or more people or groups

Use the academic words from the exercise above to complete the sentences.

4. Mary had a _____ with her brother about washing the dishes.

5. I enjoy the _____ of developing photographs.

6. Because they both liked soccer, the boys developed a strong _____.

7. Because he can cook so well, my father will _____ me with making dinner.

Complete the sentences with your own ideas.

Example: I like to assist my friends with ___*their math homework*___.

8. There was a conflict among my friends about _____.

9. I am interested in the process of _____.

10. The family member I have the closest bond with is _____

   because _____.

WORD STUDY Suffixes *-ness, -tion,* and *-ation*

Use with textbook page 87.

> **REMEMBER** A *suffix* is a letter or letters added to the end of a word to make a new word. Suffixes change the word's part of speech and meaning. Sometimes the word's spelling changes when a suffix is added, as in *note + ation = notation.*

Look at the chart. Add the suffix *-ness, -tion,* or *-ation* as directed to create a new word. Write the new word on the chart. Then write the meaning.

Word	Suffix	New Word	Definition
Example: sad	-ness	*sadness*	*unhappiness*
1. willing	-ness		
2. digest	-tion		
3. motivate	-tion		
4. reserve	-ation		
5. calculate	-ation		

Create a new word by adding the suffix *-ness, -tion,* or *-ation* to each word. Use a dictionary if needed. Then write the definition next to the new word.

Example: float ___ *+ ation = flotation   a device that helps something float* ___

6. eager ___

7. investigate ___

8. inspire ___

9. create ___

10. stipulate ___

READING STRATEGY · VISUALIZE *Use with textbook page 87.*

> **REMEMBER** When you visualize something you've read, you make a picture of it in your mind. When you read, notice descriptive words and the images the writer has created.

Read the paragraph and answer the questions that follow.

> Langston thought it was the most awesome thing he'd ever seen. The whale was blue-gray and glistening just below the surface of the water. It was so large and so close that from where he was standing, he couldn't see the head or the tail, just the massive body. It was gliding by in the water, just twenty feet from his boat. Slowly the whale started to descend into the water, the shimmering skin becoming just a dark patch. Moments later, he saw a spurt of water about 20 yards from the ship—water from the whale's blowhole. It seemed to Langston that the whale was saying goodbye.

1. What is the story about?

   _____

2. What is the strongest image in the passage?

   _____

3. What words in the passage help you to make a mental picture of the whale?

   _____

4. How can the skill of visualizing help you to understand a text more clearly?

   _____

5. Draw a picture of the scene described in the passage. Be sure to include details from the passage in your drawing.

Choose the best answer for each item. Circle the letter of the correct answer.

1. Naomi and her father bonded through _____.

   a. carving   **b.** playing games together   **c.** travelling

2. Naomi's father taught her _____.

   a. how to sell   **b.** how to cook special   **c.** how to find the magic
       his carvings   Mexican dishes   in the figurines

3. Naomi, her brother, and her grandmother leave Mexico _____.

   a. with her father   **b.** to go back to California   **c.** and move to Arizona
                                    to settle the
                                    custody problem

4. Naomi's father told her not to be sad because _____.

   a. they found each other **b.** he made her a special   **c.** they would live in
       and everything   gift to remember   Mexico
       was fine   him by

5. It is hard for Naomi to leave Mexico because _____.

   a. she hates the weather **b.** she is worried about   **c.** she doesn't want to live
       in California   her future   with her grandmother

RESPONSE TO LITERATURE *Use with textbook page 95.*

Write a few sentences explaining what you think Naomi meant by the statement
My pen seemed too heavy to lift.

_____

_____

_____

_____

_____

GRAMMAR, USAGE, AND MECHANICS

Non-action Verbs *Use with textbook page 96.*

> **REMEMBER** Non-action verbs describe conditions or situations. They express mental states (*want, need, know*), emotional states (*like, love, prefer*), possession (*have, own, belong*), sense (*taste, smell, feel, see, hear*), and other states of being (*seem, sound, look like*). Non-action verbs are mostly used in the simple present, past, or future.
> **Examples:** I need to take a nap. Megan had an old bike when she was little. I will taste some good food at the BBQ tomorrow night.

Complete each sentence with a non-action verb from the box.

has	tastes	like	knows	see

1. My cousin _____ a lot about Oaxaca.

2. Visitors _____ the friendliness of the Oaxacans.

3. Every visitor _____ the fried grasshoppers.

4. They _____ brightly painted carved animals.

5. Oaxaca _____ some of Mexico's finest beaches.

Complete each sentence with the correct form of the verb in parentheses.

Example: (want) Last summer he _____ *wanted* _____ to learn to swim.

6. (prefer) She _____ coffee ice cream to chocolate ice cream.

7. (know) By tomorrow you will _____ the whole story.

8. (sound) It _____ as if you had a great vacation.

9. (love) He _____ visiting his grandmother in Mexico last summer.

10. (belong) That book _____ to my brother.

WRITING A NARRATIVE PARAGRAPH

Write about a Character and Setting *Use with textbook page 97.*

This is the character/setting chart that Talia completed before writing her paragraph.

Character (Who)
Laura very tall, very short hair shy, plays tennis feels homesick, distraught

Setting (Where and When)
Camp Hillcrest on a beautiful hill near a huge lake first day of sleep-away camp

Complete your own chart for a paragraph about a made-up character in a realistic setting.

Character (Who)

Setting (Where and When)

UNIT 2

How does growing up change us?

READING 3: From *Later, Gator*

VOCABULARY **Literary Words** *Use with textbook page 99.*

REMEMBER **Plot** is what happens in a story. Most plots move forward in time and have a beginning, middle, and end. **Point of view** is the position from which a story is told. Some stories are told from the first-person point of view.
Example: I couldn't wait to get home.
Other stories are told from the third-person point of view.
Example: Melissa couldn't wait to get home.
The **narrator** is the person telling the story. The narrator can be a character in the story or someone telling it from the outside.

Read the passage below. Answer the questions that follow.

> Strange things happened the summer my little brother was nine. It was the craziest summer of our lives. It was also the most fun. My little brother's name is Tom. I'm David, and I'm going to tell you one unbelievable story.

1. Describe the plot of the story.

_____

2. What point of view is used in the story?

_____

3. Who is the narrator?

_____

Think of an idea for a story. What is it about? Describe the plot in the box on the left. Then write a brief description of the point of view and narrator in the box on the right.

4.	5.

Read the paragraph. Pay attention to the underlined academic words.

> I just read a book about therapy dogs, the dogs that visit patients in hospitals. A therapy dog can <u>affect</u> a patient's mood, making the patient feel happier and more hopeful. In fact, the dog's visit can have a positive <u>effect</u> on the patient's health. The <u>author</u> of the book says that not all dogs can be therapy dogs. From his <u>perspective</u>, a dog must have a calm, friendly, and outgoing personality to be a good therapy dog.

Write the academic words from the paragraph next to their correct definitions.

Example: _____*affect*_____ : do something that produces a change in someone or something; influence

1. _____ : a way of thinking about something that is influenced by the type of person you are or what you do

2. _____ : a result, or a reaction to something or someone

3. _____ : someone who writes a book, story, article, or play

Use the academic words from the paragraph to complete the sentences.

4. When Tom misbehaves in class, it has an _____ on everyone.

5. How much sleep I get will _____ my mood.

6. When it comes to teamwork, Jana has a different _____ than everyone else because she is used to working alone.

7. Mark is such a good writer, he could be a successful _____ .

Complete the sentences with your own ideas.

Example: A book or movie that had an effect on me was ___*The Black Stallion*___ .

8. When I don't complete my homework on time, it can affect _____ .

9. When people want to hear my perspective on something, I feel

_____ .

10. I like it when an author writes about _____ .

WORD STUDY Animal Verbs and Idioms *Use with textbook page 101.*

REMEMBER Idioms are phrases that cannot be taken literally, such as "Lisa's boyfriend is in the dog house" to mean "Lisa is angry at her boyfriend." Use animal idioms to make your writing vivid, descriptive, and humorous.

Look at the chart below. Write the meaning of each animal idiom. Use a dictionary if needed.

Animal Idiom	Meaning
That boy has ants in his pants!	*The boy can't sit still.*
1. You are barking up the wrong tree.	
2. The mechanic is busy as a beaver.	
3. This movie is for the birds.	
4. They are dropping like flies.	

Rewrite each animal idiom in your own words to explain its meaning. Use a dictionary if needed.

Example: Edmundo is like a bull in a china shop. ___*Edmundo is very clumsy.*___

5. He was a wolf in sheep's clothing. _____

6. Don't bug me! _____

7. Her bark is worse than her bite. _____

8. She has eagle eyes. _____

9. The boss is a fat cat. _____

10. He's a lucky dog. _____

REMEMBER When you read a story, pay attention to the sequence of events (the order in which they occur) to help you understand the plot.

Read the paragraphs and answer the questions that follow.

There are live volcanoes all over the earth and when they erupt, they can cause great damage. Some have small eruptions while others, like Mt. St. Helens in Washington State, have large eruptions. Mt. St. Helens erupted on Sunday, May 18, 1980.

Volcanoes are caused by hot lava below the earth's crust, called magma, breaking through the surface. When a volcano erupts, first the ground shakes. Next, ash, gas and rock blow through the top or side of the volcano. Parts of the volcano may collapse. Then, lava pours out, flowing down the sides. Finally, over time, the hot lava cools, and turns to rock.

1. What specific event is mentioned in the passage?

_____

2. How does the sequence of events begin in the passage?

_____

3. Use the chart. What is the correct sequence of events of a volcano erupting?

First	Next	Then	Finally

4. What happens at the end of the passage?

_____

5. How does the skill of identifying sequence help you to understand a text?

_____

COMPREHENSION   *Use with textbook page 108.*

Choose the best answer for each item. Circle the letter of the correct answer.

1. Last Christmas, Teddy gave Bobby socks because _____.

   a. he needed socks

   b. he didn't want to give Bobby something he wanted

   c. he didn't have enough money to buy him something else

2. Teddy's mother wants him _____.

   a. to give Bobby something special

   b. to do all Bobby's chores

   c. to cook the birthday breakfast

3. Teddy wants to get Bobby an alligator so _____.

   a. he can play with it too

   b. he can keep his promise to his mother and horrify Bobby

   c. Bobby will have the pet he's always wanted

4. The narrator of the story is _____.

   a. the mother

   b. Bobby

   c. Teddy

5. When Teddy describes Bobby as a "walking Hallmark card," he means Bobby

   is _____.

   a. funny

   b. cute

   c. too nice

RESPONSE TO LITERATURE   *Use with textbook page 109.*

Imagine what will happen next in the story as it continues. How do you think the story will end? Write an ending for the story on the lines below.

_____

_____

_____

_____

_____

GRAMMAR, USAGE, AND MECHANICS

Making Comparisons *Use with textbook page 110.*

> **REMEMBER** Comparative adjectives compare two things. Add *-r* or *-er* to form the comparative of a one-syllable adjective.
> **Example:** Your backyard is larger than mine.
> To form the comparative of a two-syllable adjective ending in *-y*, change the *y* to *i* and add *-er*.
> **Example:** This movie is funnier than the one we watched last night.
> To form the comparative of an adjective that has two or more syllables and does not end in *-y*, use *more . . . than* or *less . . . than*.
> **Example:** Calculus is more complicated than regular math.
> To show that two things are equal or unequal, use *as . . . as* or *not as . . . as*.
> **Example:** I am just as pleased as you are that our cousins are coming to visit.

Complete each sentence with the correct form of the adjective in parentheses.

Example: (cheap) The blue shirt is _____ *cheaper* _____ than the white one.

1. (famous) No other president is as _____ as George Washington.

2. (polite) The obedient girl was _____ than her playful sister.

3. (easy) It is _____ to buy a cake than to make one.

Write sentences with comparative adjectives. Follow the directions in parentheses and use the correct form of the adjective.

Example: (Use *strong + than* to say that one thing or person has less strength than the other.)

   Plywood is less strong than solid wood. _____

4. (Use *honest + as . . . as* to say that two people are equally honest.)

   _____

5. (Use *hopeful + than* to say that one person has more hope than another.)

   _____

WRITING a NARRATIVE PARAGRAPH

Write a Story from Another Point of View *Use with textbook page 111.*

This is the T-chart that Koji completed before writing his paragraph.

Teddy's POV	Mother's POV
Bobby drives me crazy!	*Teddy's jealous of Bobby.*
I saw: BABY ALLIGATORS ON SALE. Mother had said to buy Bobby a pet.	*I told Teddy to buy Bobby something special. I thought a little turtle would be a wonderful gift.*
Bobby would run shrieking from the room.	*I found a baby alligator in the turtle bowl. I shrieked.*
Mother would learn her lesson.	*I should have guessed that Teddy would outsmart me.*

Complete your own T-chart contrasting the perspectives of the original narrator from a familiar story and another character's point of view.

Familiar Point of View	New Point of View

How does growing up change us?

READING 4: "Amazing Growth Facts" /
"The Old Grandfather and His Little Grandson"

VOCABULARY **Key Words** *Use with textbook page 113.*

Write each word in the box next to its definition.

average	conversion	height	length	rate	weight

Example: _____*average*_____ : having qualities that are typical of most people or things

1. _____ : when you change something from one form, system, or
   purpose to another

2. _____ : the measurement of something from one end to another

3. _____ : the number of times something happens over a period
   of time

4. _____ : how heavy someone or something is

5. _____ : how tall someone or something is

Use the words in the box at the top of the page to complete the sentences.

6. I use a _____ chart to change miles to kilometers.

7. When I went to the doctor, she measured my _____ with a
   tape measure.

8. When I measured the _____ of the hallway, I discovered that it was
   longer than I had expected.

9. I am tall for my age; my mom says my height is above _____.

10. My hair grows at a very fast _____.

VOCABULARY   **Academic Words** *Use with textbook page 114.*

Read the paragraph below. Pay attention to the underlined academic words.

> It's important to eat plenty of foods from the fruit and vegetable <u>category</u> of the food chart. One major <u>benefit</u> of eating fruits and vegetables is all the vitamins they give you. For example, broccoli contains an <u>enormous</u> amount of vitamin C. Just one serving of broccoli contains 220 <u>percent</u> of the recommended daily allowance of vitamin C.

Write the letter of the correct definition next to each word.

Example: ___c___ benefit

_____ 1. category

_____ 2. percent

_____ 3. enormous

a. equal to a particular amount in every hundred

b. extremely large in size or amount

c. something that gives you an advantage, that helps you, or that has a good effect

d. group of people or things that have related characteristics

Use the academic words from the exercise above to complete the sentences.

4. The treasurer had a _____ for each type of expense.

5. On her way to school, Ann Marie saw an _____ bird that looked like a hawk.

6. Extra help with my science project will be a huge _____ to me.

7. I was glad when 60 _____ of the students supported my brother for class president.

Complete the sentences with your own ideas.

Example: I am in the same age category as ___*my friend Alicia*___.

8. An enormous challenge I have faced is _____.

9. The benefit of going to school is _____.

10. I agreed with my friend one hundred percent when he said

_____.

Use with textbook page 115.

REMEMBER The long /ō/ can be spelled in many ways, including *o* as in *hold*, *o_e* as in *bone*, *oa* as in *oak*, and *ow* as in *blow*. Knowing these four patterns can help you spell many words with the long /ō/ correctly.

Read the words in the box. Then write each word in the correct column in the chart.

| robot | below | goat | cone | pillow | joke |
| coast | soda | grove | shallow | roast | host |

/ō/ spelled *o*	/ō/ spelled *o_e*	/ō/ spelled *oa*	/ō/ spelled *ow*
robot			

Write the spelling of long /ō/ in each word.

Example: toast _____ /ō/ spelled oa _____

1. mold _____

2. zone _____

3. flown _____

4. gloat _____

5. sold _____

6. grown _____

7. bow _____

8. vote _____

9. role _____

Name _____ Date _____

Use with textbook page 115.

> **REMEMBER** You use visuals in a text to help you understand what is happening. Visuals can be charts, maps, photographs, drawings, or diagrams.

Look at the pictures and text and answer the questions that follow.

Adult Animals and Their Eggs

Egg Size No Indication of Adult Size

The Golden Eagle has an egg the same size as that of the Nile Crocodile. But while the adult Golden Eagle only reaches 88 cm when full grown, the Nile Crocodile will grow to 5 meters!

U.S. Units

It is easier to understand how big the eggs and animals are if we convert their sizes into U.S. units. Take a look at the chart to see how the measurement rates compare.

Conversion Chart		
Metric		**U.S. Customary Units**
1 millimeter	=	0.039 inch
1 centimeter	=	0.39 inch
1 meter	=	3.28 feet
1 gram	=	0.035 ounce
1 kilogram	=	2.2 pounds

1. What do you think the article is about?

_____

2. How do the pictures help you to understand the text?

_____

3. How does the chart help you to understand the text?

_____

4. What is one thing you learned from the information given?

_____

5. How do you think the skill of using visuals can help you to understand the text?

_____

Choose the best answer for each item. Circle the letter of the correct answer.

1. One of the longest living creatures is the _____.

   a. eagle   **b.** human   **c.** clam

2. As children, boys and girls are usually about the same _____.

   a. weight, but not height   **b.** height, but not weight   **c.** height and weight

3. An ant can lift more than one hundred times its _____.

   a. rate   **b.** weight   **c.** height

4. The average human life span is about _____.

   a. 70 years   **b.** 50 years   **c.** 100 years

5. All living things _____ in size.

   a. decrease   **b.** increase   **c.** fall

EXTENSION *Use with textbook page 121.*

The folk tale "The Old Grandfather and His Little Grandson" is a reminder that you should treat people with care and respect. You should treat people the way you wish to be treated. Write a sentence describing how you like to be treated. Write a sentence about how you do not like to be treated.

I like to be treated:

_____

_____

I do not like to be treated:

_____

_____

Name _____ Date _____

GRAMMAR, USAGE, AND MECHANICS

Simple Past: Regular and Irregular verbs *Use with textbook page 122.*

REMEMBER The simple past describes completed actions or conditions in the past. Form the simple past of regular verbs by adding *-d* or *-ed* to the base form.
Example: I walked to the zoo yesterday.
If a verb ends in a consonant, sometimes you must double the final consonant before you add *-ed*.
Example: I nodded to my sister to tell her I was ready to go.
If a verb ends in a consonant and *-y*, change the *y* to *i* and add *-ed*.
Example: I hurried to make it to school on time.
If a verb ends in a vowel and *y*, just add *-ed*.
Example: I annoyed my sister when I teased her about her new haircut.
The past form of many common verbs is irregular. Those forms must be memorized.
Example: I went to the amusement park with my aunt and uncle.

Complete each sentence with a verb from the box.

weighed	enjoyed	was	carried	chopped

1. He _____ the groceries home from the store.

2. The bicycle _____ in the garage.

3. The package _____ five pounds.

4. The cook _____ the vegetables.

5. Everyone _____ the meal.

Complete each sentence with the simple past of the verb in parentheses.

Example: (lift) The athlete _____*lifted*_____ the weight.

6. (let) She _____ the dog play in the field.

7. (say) The announcer _____ a few words.

8. (be) His friends _____ on the playground.

9. (fry) My father _____ the fish.

10. (bob) The toy boat _____ up and down in the water.

Write a Personal Narrative *Use with textbook page 123.*

This is the sequence-of-events chart that Brandon completed before writing his paragraph.

> **Beginning**
> *I went to my abuelo's house. He asked me to help him learn how to use the computer.*

↓

> **Middle**
> *I showed him how to turn on the Internet, find a Spanish newspaper, and turn the computer off.*

↓

> **End**
> *Abuelo is now able to show other people how to use the Internet.*

Complete your own sequence-of-events chart for a personal narrative.

> **Beginning**
>
>
>

↓

> **Middle**
>
>
>

↓

> **End**
>
>
>

EDIT AND PROOFREAD   *Use with textbook page 130.*

Read the paragraph below carefully. Look for mistakes in spelling, punctuation, and grammar. Mark the mistakes with proofreader's marks (textbook page 454). Then rewrite the paragraph correctly on the lines below.

> Yesterday, my dad asked me to watch my little Sister amy while he went to the store. "Sure, I said. Amy is three years old. Usually I think shes cute, but not today. As soon as our dad left, Amy throwed her crackers on the kitchen floor. She spiled her juice on purpose. She dumped out a box of cereal. When I asked her to clean it up, she laughed and ran into the other room. After I cleaned up the crackers juice, and cerael, I went to find Amy. She was in my room tearing up my favorite magazine. "Amy, stop!" I yelled. Just then my Dad came home "Thanks for watching Amy. Will you watch her again tomorrow?" he asked. "No way!" I said

_____

_____

_____

_____

_____

_____

_____

_____

_____

_____

_____

_____

Underline the vocabulary items you know and can use well. Review and practice any you haven't underlined. Underline them when you know them well.

Literary Words	Key Words	Academic Words	
dialogue	ancient	classical	affect
setting	ceremony	cultural	author
plot	citizen	feature	effect
point of view	education	philosophy	perspective
narrator	rights	assist	benefit
	rituals	bond	category
	average	conflict	enormous
	conversion	process	percent
	height		
	length		
	rate		
	weight		

Put a check by the skills you can perform well. Review and practice any you haven't checked off. Check them off when you can perform them well.

Skills	I can . . .
Word Study	☐ spell words with the long vowel sound /ē/. ☐ recognize and use suffixes *-ness*, *-tion*, and *-ation*. ☐ recognize and use animal verbs and idioms. ☐ spell words with the long vowel sound /ō/.
Reading Strategies	☐ compare and contrast. ☐ visualize. ☐ recognize sequence. ☐ use visuals.
Grammar, Usage, and Mechanics	☐ show contrast using transitions and coordinating conjunctions. ☐ use non-action verbs. ☐ make comparisons. ☐ use simple past with regular and irregular verbs.
Writing	☐ write a friendly letter. ☐ write about a character and setting. ☐ write a story from another point of view. ☐ write a personal narrative. ☐ write a fictional narrative.

Learn about Art with the Smithsonian
American Art Museum *Use with textbook pages 132–133.*

LEARNING TO LOOK

Look at *The Lost Balloon* by William Holbrook Beard on page 133. Use that artwork to complete the web diagram below. For each "string" coming from the center, list one observation about the artwork.

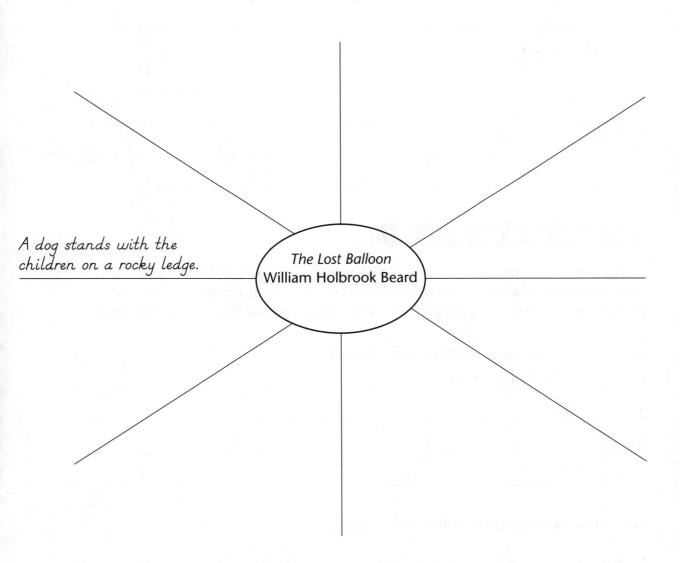

A dog stands with the children on a rocky ledge.

The Lost Balloon
William Holbrook Beard

Look at *The Lost Balloon* by William Holbrook Beard again. Pretend you are one of the children in the painting.

What are you doing?

_____

_____

_____

_____

What do you see?

_____

_____

_____

_____

COMPARE & CONTRAST

Look at *Child on a Rocking Horse* by Albert Bisbee on page 132. Find a photograph of yourself or of someone you know. Compare the face of the girl in Bisbee's photograph with the face of the person (perhaps you!) in the other photograph.

Write down three ways that they are different.

Example: ___*My face is larger.*_____.

1. _____

2. _____

3. _____

Write down three ways that they are similar.

4. _____

5. _____

6. _____

How does helping others help us all?

READING 1: From *Run Away Home*

VOCABULARY **Literary Words** *Use with textbook page 137.*

> **REMEMBER** Writers use **dialect** to show how people speak in a specific region. Often, writers create a **mood** or feeling in a story. One mood is **suspense**, which is uncertainty about what will happen.

Read each sentence. Write *Dialect* if the sentence contains dialect. Write *Mood* if the sentence has a mood. Write *Suspense* if the sentence contains suspense.

Dialect, Mood, or Suspense	Sentence
Mood	It was a dark, dreary night that made us feel sad.
1.	The heavy footsteps came nearer and nearer and stopped outside my room.
2.	"But of course you'd druther work, I reckon," Tom Sawyer said.
3.	Hector opened the big gift slowly as we all held our breath.
4.	The sun shone brightly, the birds sang sweetly, and the clouds looked like cotton candy.
5.	Huck said, "Oh, don't be afeared b'cause we ain't causin' no harm."

Read the story "The Big Test." Six parts are underlined. Label each underlined part as Suspense, Dialect, or Mood. The first example is done for you.

Mood

It was a gloomy and depressing winter day. Everyone in class waited to hear what Ms. Chin the teacher would say. Ms. Chin just stared at the class. The ticking clock sounded — 8. very loud.

6. Finally, Rita said, "Ma'am, do you'all know how we did on the big test?"

9.

Still Ms. Chin said nothing. The kids held their breath. Some felt like they were going to scream with the tension!

7. Brad said, "Gollee! Pleeze tell us already!"

10.

"You all passed!" Mrs. Chin shouted. The kids smiled in joy and cheered happily.

Read the paragraph below. Pay attention to the underlined academic words.

There are no <u>precise</u> rules about how to thank someone for a gift. However, it is important that you <u>communicate</u> your appreciation for the gift as soon as possible. If you are sending a thank-you note, it's most <u>appropriate</u> to send it the first week after receiving the gift. It is considered rude to let an extended <u>period</u> of time pass before sending a thank-you note.

Write the academic words from the paragraph above next to their correct definitions.

Example: ___*appropriate*___ : suitable for a particular time, situation, or purpose

1. _____ : a particular length of time in history or in a person's life

2. _____ : exact and correct in every detail

3. _____ : express your thoughts and feelings so that others understand them

Use the academic words from the paragraph above to complete the sentences.

4. People _____ with movements as well as words.

5. It is _____ to carry an umbrella when it is likely to rain.

6. Julio's watch is _____ , so he always arrives on time.

7. The nineteenth century was a _____ of great progress in America.

Complete the sentences with your own ideas.

Example: I like to communicate with ___*email and text messages*___ .

8. My favorite period of American history is _____ .

9. I think it is important to be precise about _____ .

10. It is appropriate to buy a gift when _____ .

WORD STUDY   Uses of the Apostrophe *Use with textbook page 139.*

> **REMEMBER** An apostrophe is used to show where letters have been left out in a contraction. For example, the words *I* and *am* can be shortened to form the contraction *I'm*. An apostrophe is also used in dialect to show where letters are missing, as in the expression *yo'* for *you*.

Look at the chart below. Form the contraction for each pair of words. Write the contraction in the chart.

Word #1	Word #2	Contraction
would	not	*wouldn't*
1. you	will	
2. are	not	
3. who	is	
4. we	are	
5. she	is	

Look at the chart below. Write the word that each example of dialect represents. The dialect is underlined.

Dialect	Word
6. 'Deed, I do believe what you say is true.	
7. What are you thinkin' of doing now?	
8. Take off your gloves and put 'em down.	
9. I have had 'bout enough of your tricks!	
10. I s'pose I could help you out tomorrow.	

REMEMBER When you read, make inferences by trying to understand what the author means but does not say directly. Use clues in the text and your own experiences to make inferences.

Read each paragraph and answer the questions that follow.

Rob had been playing hockey since he was 5. He dreamed of being named captain of the team. He practiced all winter long. When the coach announced that another player would be captain of the team, Rob was upset. The coach said, "Rob—you're still an important player on the team." Rob replied, "I only cared about being captain. Now I'm not sure I even want to play."

1. What can you infer about Rob's character from the passage above?

_____

_____

2. What clues in the text helped you to make an inference about Rob's character?

_____

_____

Rita and Mia were working on a science project together. They agreed to split the work in half and each do their part. When the project was due, Rita had completed hers, but Mia had not even started hers. Mia said, "Well, we can tell the teacher that we both completed the first half of the project and then ran out of time."

3. What can you infer about Mia's character from the passage above?

_____

_____

4. What clues in the text helped you to make an inference about Mia's character?

_____

_____

5. How do you think making inferences can help you to read with better comprehension?

_____

_____

Name _____ Date _____

Choose the best answer for each item. Circle the letter of the correct answer.

1. Sky is ill because he has _____.

   a. swamp fever   **b.** quinine   **c.** many mosquito bites

2. Sky escaped because _____.

   a. he wants to leave   **b.** he didn't want to   **c.** he had to find
      the country   go to school   his family
                       in Pennsylvania

3. The message *the quilt is torn* means that _____.

   a. Sky ran away   **b.** Sky got better   **c.** Sky died

4. Mr. Wratten wants to help Sky because _____.

   a. he feels sorry   **b.** he will get money   **c.** he is his father
      for him

5. Papa gets Sky to _____.

   a. eat all the pork   **b.** tell the truth   **c.** act with respect
                   about his past

RESPONSE TO LITERATURE *Use with textbook page 147.*

Write a paragraph that tells what you think will happen next in the story. Use dialogue to show the speaker's exact words. Write at least five lines.

_____

_____

_____

_____

_____

_____

_____

_____

GRAMMAR, USAGE, AND MECHANICS

Simple and Compound Sentences *Use with textbook page 148.*

> **REMEMBER** A sentence is a group of words that expresses a complete thought. A simple sentence has one subject and one verb.
> **Example:** The boy spoke.
> A compound sentence contains two simple sentences joined by a coordinating conjunction *(and, but, or or)*.
> **Example:** The boy spoke, and the girl answered.
> In a compound sentence, there is usually a comma before the coordinating conjunction.

Identify each sentence by writing *simple* or *compound* next to it.

Example: ___*simple*___ The student wrote the sentence correctly.

_____ **1.** The woman coughed.

_____ **2.** The boy hummed a song, but the girl only mumbled.

_____ **3.** The child whispered to the adult.

_____ **4.** The man yawned, and his wife sighed.

_____ **5.** Throughout the day, either the turtle snapped, or the dog yelped.

Form a compound sentence by writing a simple sentence after each coordinating conjunction.

Example: The man was unkind, but ___*later he apologized.*___

6. Mom hides our gifts in the closet, or _____

7. Teachers teach lessons, and _____

8. The soup smells good, but _____

9. The guests will leave soon, or _____

10. An explorer tries new things, and _____

WRITING a PERSUASIVE PARAGRAPH

Write a Book Review *Use with textbook page 149.*

This is the opinion-reasons chart that Danielle completed before writing her book review.

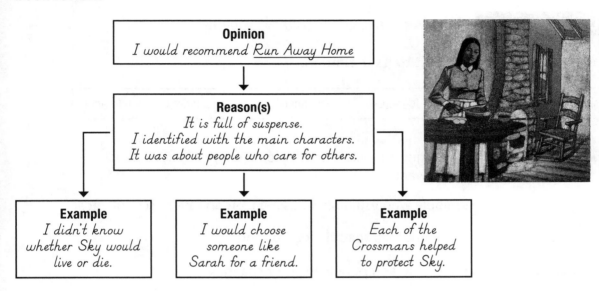

Opinion
I would recommend Run Away Home

↓

Reason(s)
It is full of suspense.
I identified with the main characters.
It was about people who care for others.

Example
I didn't know whether Sky would live or die.

Example
I would choose someone like Sarah for a friend.

Example
Each of the Crossmans helped to protect Sky.

Complete your own opinion-reasons chart for a review of a book or story that you like very much.

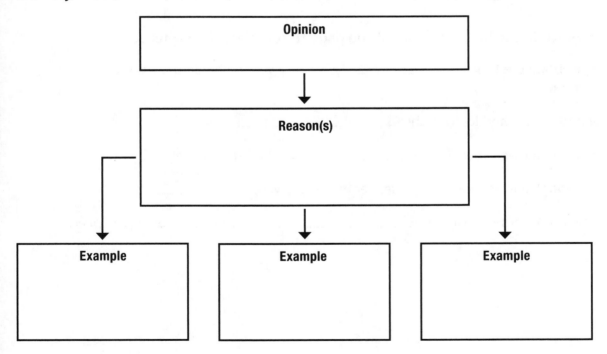

Opinion

↓

Reason(s)

Example

Example

Example

UNIT 3

How does helping others help us all?

READING 2: "Extraordinary People: Serving Others"

VOCABULARY **Key Words** *Use with textbook page 151.*

Write each word in the box next to its definition.

assassinated	extraordinary	founders	resistance	superintendent	tolerance

Example: ___*tolerance*___: willingness to allow people to do, say, or believe what they want

1. _____: people who establish a business, organization, school, etc.

2. _____: very unusual, special, or surprising

3. _____: refusal to accept new ideas or changes

4. _____: murdered (an important person)

5. _____: someone who is responsible for a place, job, activity, etc.

Use the words in the box at the top of the page to complete the sentences.

6. We celebrate the town _____ every year by holding a parade in their honor.

7. The motto "live and let live" shows _____.

8. The mules showed their _____ by refusing to move!

9. World War I started when a royal leader in Europe was _____.

10. Comic book heroes always have _____ powers, such as super speed.

Name _____ Date _____

Read the paragraph below. Pay attention to the underlined academic words.

My soccer coach has played a positive <u>role</u> in my life. He helped me <u>alter</u> my exercise and practice routine. The changes made a strong <u>impact</u> on my soccer skills. I was named team captain by mid-season. My coach helped me <u>achieve</u> this goal.

Write the letter of the correct definition next to each word.

Example: ___c___ achieve

_____ **1.** alter

_____ **2.** impact

_____ **3.** role

a. change in some way

b. the position, job, or function someone or something has in a particular situation or activity

c. succeed in doing or getting something as a result of your actions

d. the effect that something or someone has on someone or something

Use the academic words from the exercise above to complete the sentences.

4. The weather has a big _____ on her feelings.

5. John has a starring _____ in the play.

6. One of the best ways to _____ your goals is through hard work.

7. Rick can never decide what to do, so he will often _____ his plans at the last minute.

Complete the sentences with your own ideas.

Example: Pets can play an important role in __*helping blind people*__.

8. The person who has had the biggest impact on my life is

_____.

9. One thing I would like to alter about my daily life is

_____.

10. The goals I plan to achieve include _____.

Use with textbook page 153.

WORD STUDY Spelling Words with Silent *gh*

REMEMBER In English, the letters *gh* are often silent, but not always. For example, the letters *gh* are silent in the word *though*, but they stand for the sound /g/ in the word *ghostly*. Knowing when the letters *gh* are silent will help you spell and pronounce words correctly.

Read the words in the box below. Then write each word in the correct column in the chart.

weight	spaghetti	ghost	straight	gherkin
tight	ghetto	ghastly	through	ought

Silent *gh*	*gh* stands for /g/
weight	

Write "silent gh" next to the words that have a silent *gh*. Write "/g/" next to any words in which the letters *gh* stand for the sound /g/.

Example: though _____*silent gh*_____

1. slight _____

2. slaughter _____

3. Ghana _____

4. thigh _____

5. eight _____

6. high _____

READING STRATEGY | IDENTIFY PROBLEMS AND SOLUTIONS

Use with textbook page 153.

> **REMEMBER** When you read, try to identify problems and solutions. A problem is a challenge that a person, group, or character faces. A solution is how the person, group, or character fixes the problem.

Read each paragraph. Then answer the questions that follow.

Gemma forgot her lunch money. She had no idea how she was going to pay for lunch. She called her parents but they couldn't come to school and bring her money. Then her best friend offered to share her lunch with Gemma. There was more than enough for both of them.

1. What is the problem in the passage above?

_____

_____

2. What is the solution in the passage above?

_____

_____

Oscar was failing at science class. He found it very difficult and did not know what to do. Then the science teacher offered to tutor him after class. Oscar worked with his science teacher, and in a few weeks, his grades were much better.

3. What is the problem in the passage above?

_____

_____

4. What is the solution to the problem?

_____

_____

5. How do you think the strategy of identifying a problem and a solution will make you a better reader?

_____

_____

Choose the best answer for each item. Circle the letter of the correct answer.

1. Benito Juárez is famous for _____.

   a. starting a nursing school

   b. serving as a president of Mexico who made many reforms

   c. using passive resistance

2. Florence Nightingale was called _____.

   a. "mother to millions"

   b. "England's helper"

   c. "the lady with the lamp"

3. The international symbol of nonviolent protest is _____.

   a. Doctors without Borders

   b. Mohandas Gandhi

   c. Helen Keller

4. Franklin Delano Roosevelt is ranked as one of America's greatest presidents because _____.

   a. he helped the nation through very difficult times

   b. he started hospitals

   c. he had polio

5. Helen Keller is celebrated today for _____.

   a. leading nations

   b. giving medical care

   c. inspiring handicapped people

EXTENSION *Use with textbook page 159.*

Think about famous people you have heard about. Write why they are famous and why you admire them.

Person or Group	Why Famous	Why I Admire the Person

GRAMMAR, USAGE, AND MECHANICS

Prepositions of Time: *in, on,* and *at* *Use with textbook page 160.*

REMEMBER The prepositions *in, on,* and *at* refer to points in time. Use *in* before months, years, centuries, and seasons.
Examples: in May; in 1776; in the twenty-first century; in winter
Use *on* before days and exact dates.
Examples: on Tuesday; on July 4
Use *at* before times of day.
Example: at nine o'clock

Complete the chart with items from the box. Write each word or phrase under the preposition it's used with.

June	midnight	Monday	Thanksgiving	the summer
March 4	8:15 A.M.	the tenth century	seven o'clock	1984

in		
1.	3.	
2.	4.	

on	at
5.	8.
6.	9.
7.	10.

Complete each sentence with *in, on,* or *at.*

Example: The United States won its independence _____*in*_____ the eighteenth century.

11. The United States declared its independence _____ July 4, 1776.

12. We observe the birthday of Martin Luther King Jr. _____ January.

13. The movie will be on television tonight _____ eight o'clock.

14. The new year begins _____ midnight.

15. Thanksgiving is always celebrated _____ a Thursday.

WRITING A PERSUASIVE PARAGRAPH

Use a Question-and-Answer Format *Use with textbook page 161.*

This is the question-and-answer chart that Tamar completed before writing her question-and-answer paragraph.

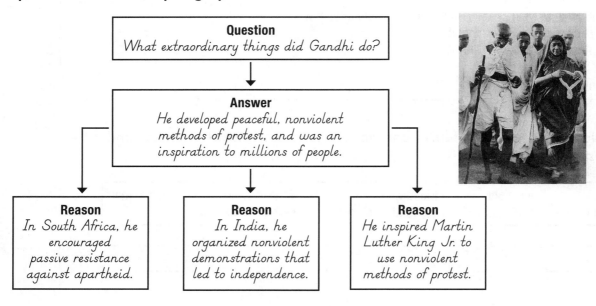

Complete your own question-and-answer chart for a paragraph about someone you think is truly extraordinary. Answer the question *"What extraordinary things did this person do?"*

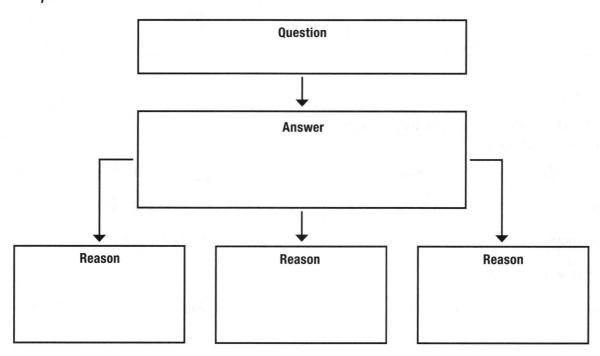

Name _____ Date _____

How does helping others help us all?

READING 3: From *Zlata's Diary*

VOCABULARY **Literary Words** *Use with textbook page 163.*

REMEMBER A **figure of speech** is a group of words or phrases that do not match the literal, or dictionary definition, of the words.
Example: The steak was as tough as nails.
Hyperbole is a figure of speech that uses exaggeration, or overstatement.
Example: I'm so hungry that I could eat a whole cow!

Read each sentence. Write *figure of speech* if the sentence has a figure of speech. If the figure of speech is a hyperbole, write *hyperbole*.

Literary Words	Sentence
hyperbole	The joke was so funny that José nearly died laughing.
1.	The math test was as easy as pie.
2.	The model wore at least 100 pounds of makeup.
3.	It's 1,000 degrees outside.
4.	I'm so tired that I could sleep for a year.
5.	That sofa cost an arm and a leg.

Write sentences using the literary elements listed.

Literary Element	Sentence
Figure of speech	*Jack is always pulling our leg with his jokes.*
6. Hyperbole	
7. Figure of speech	
8. Hyperbole	
9. Figure of speech	
10. Hyperbole	

Read the paragraph below. Pay attention to the underlined academic words.

All of us suffer from <u>stress</u> at times. Experts say that the best <u>method</u> for fighting stress is to <u>establish</u> a healthy lifestyle. The basics of a healthy lifestyle include a diet that should <u>consist</u> of healthy, balanced foods, at least one hour of exercise a day, and between seven and nine hours of sleep a night.

Write the academic words from the paragraph above next to their correct definitions.

Example: _____*stress*_____: continuous feelings of worry caused by difficulties in your life

1. _____: are made up of or contain particular things or people

2. _____: create; organize

3. _____: a planned way of doing something

Use the academic words from the paragraph above to complete the sentences.

4. I always feel _____ before a big test.

5. The class wants to _____ a scholarship fund.

6. Luis has his own _____ for raking leaves.

7. The meal will _____ of foods from many countries.

Complete the sentences with your own ideas.

Example: I feel stress when ____*I oversleep in the morning*____.

8. My birthday party will consist of _____.

9. I would like to establish a club that _____.

10. My method for cleaning my room is _____.

WORD STUDY · Synonyms and Antonyms *Use with textbook page 165.*

> **REMEMBER** Synonyms are words with the same or nearly the same meaning, such as *error* and *mistake*. Antonyms are words that have opposite or nearly opposite meanings, such as *hot* and *cold*. You can use context clues, including synonyms and antonyms, to figure out words that you don't know.

Read the sentences in the chart below. Underline the context clues that help you figure out the meaning of each boldfaced word. Then identify the type of the clue you found. Write the clue word in the second column of the chart, and label it *synonym* or *antonym*.

Sentences with Unfamiliar Words	Type of Context Clue
During the war, everyday items that once were <u>cheap</u> became very **expensive**.	*cheap = antonym*
1. Zlata felt very unsafe during the war. She and her family faced many **hazardous** situations.	
2. Neighbors who were friends a year ago are now **enemies**.	
3. In order to **defend** ourselves, we had to know when the bombers were going to attack.	
4. During the war, I read newspapers because I wanted to know the facts. I didn't want to read any **fiction**.	
5. The bridge was **damaged** during the conflict, but later it was repaired.	

Read each sentence. Underline words or phrases that are clues to meaning. Then write your own definition of each boldfaced term.

Example: Although I **nagged** him, he was never <u>annoyed</u> by my questions.

   nagged = asked annoying questions

6. Today the ocean is calm again; it looks as **tranquil** as a sheet of glass.

_____

7. The market is **bustling** from Monday to Friday, but it is quiet on the weekend.

_____

8. My sister has no sense of **decorum**. Her rude behavior upsets me.

_____

Use with textbook page 165.

> **REMEMBER** When you read, distinguish fact from opinion. A fact is a statement that can be proven. An opinion is a person's point of view about a topic. Opinions are not necessarily wrong, but they can't be proven.

Read each pair of statements. Then answer the questions that follow.

Carrots are full of vitamins. I think they taste great.

1. Which statement is a fact?

   _____

   _____

2. Which statement is an opinion?

   _____

   _____

Flowers come in many colors. I love them!

3. Which statement is a fact?

   _____

   _____

4. Which statement is an opinion?

   _____

   _____

5. How can the strategy of distinguishing between fact and opinion help you become a better reader?

   _____

   _____

   _____

   _____

COMPREHENSION   *Use with textbook page 172.*

Choose the best answer for each item. Circle the letter of the correct answer.

1. Zlata's diary is about _____.

   a. only herself   **b.** her mother "Mimmy"   **c.** the war in Sarajevo

2. In her entry on May 26, Zlata wants to _____.

   a. move away for good   **b.** learn to speak English   **c.** give her friend a
                                                                        birthday gift

3. Vaso Miskin Street is _____.

   a. the scene of many   **b.** where Zlata lives   **c.** where Zlata's dad
   bombs and death   works

4. As winter comes to the town, people _____.

   a. celebrate peace   **b.** lack water and electricity **c.** play games with kids

5. Zlata's parents _____.

   a. get thin and sad   **b.** decide to get new jobs   **c.** play the piano for fun

RESPONSE TO LITERATURE   *Use with textbook page 173.*

Read the dates from Zlata's diary. First read what happened each day. Then write what you might do or how you might feel if you were in Zlata's place.

Saturday
May 23   _____

Tuesday
May 26   _____

Wednesday
May 27   _____

Thursday
October 1   _____

Monday
December 28   _____

GRAMMAR, USAGE, AND MECHANICS

Placement of Adjectives *Use with textbook page 174.*

> **REMEMBER** An adjective describes a noun. It can appear before the noun.
> **Example:** That is a big dog.
> It can also appear after a linking verb. A linking verb describes a state of being. *Get, become, seem, appear, feel, taste, sound, smell, look,* and forms of *be* are all linking verbs.
> **Example:** That dog is big.

Complete each sentence with an adjective from the box.

first	brown	warm	true	disappointed

1. Everything the girl wrote was _____.

2. After losing, the _____ players promised to win the next game.

3. Tomorrow is the _____ day of spring.

4. The _____ dog ran across the yard.

5. The stove still feels _____.

Write sentences with adjectives. Use the words in parentheses.

Example: (*be happy.*)

   Everyone is happy.

6. (*two friends*)

   _____

7. (*quiet street*)

   _____

8. (*wonderful surprise*)

   _____

9. (*seem sad*)

   _____

10. (*look cheerful*)

   _____

WRITING A PERSUASIVE PARAGRAPH

Write a Diary Entry *Use with textbook page 175.*

This is the T-chart that Talia completed before writing her paragraph.

ISSUE	
Is nonviolence a better way to solve problems than violence?	
For	**Against**
Innocent people like Zlata and her family suffer during war.	*The only way to confront violence is with more violence.*
Peaceful protest sends a powerful message and is less likely to harm others.	

Complete your own T-chart for a diary entry about an important issue in the world.

ISSUE	
For	**Against**

How does helping others help us all?

READING 4: "Friendship and Cooperation in the Animal Kingdom"

VOCABULARY **Key Words** *Use with textbook page 177.*

Write each word in the box next to its definition.

arrangement	cooperate	damage	gigantic	intruder	tsunami

Example: ___*tsunami*___ : a very large ocean wave caused by an underwater earthquake

1. _____ : physical harm that is done to something

2. _____ : work together with someone else to achieve something

3. _____ : extremely large

4. _____ : something that has been organized or agreed on

5. _____ : someone who enters an area where he or she is not supposed to be

Use the words in the box at the top of the page to complete the sentences.

6. When we _____, our chores get done faster because everyone helps out.

7. Dolphins are small, not _____.

8. The _____ looked like a wall of water crashing down on the village.

9. My mother has a(n) _____ with a neighbor who takes in our mail.

10. Any crash will _____ a car.

VOCABULARY **Academic Words** *Use with textbook page 178.*

Read the paragraph below. Pay attention to the underlined academic words.

> The World Kindness Movement was formed in 1997 by a group in Japan who wanted to spread the <u>concept</u> of kindness. They believe that having a positive <u>attitude</u> and doing kind things for others can help improve a community. Acts of kindness can be as simple as thanking the people we <u>rely on</u> every day, such as firemen and policemen. One may <u>comment</u> that being nice isn't so hard, and the World Kindness Movement hopes that everyone sees it that way.

Write the letter of the correct definition next to each word.

Example: ___*b*___ rely on

_____ **1.** concept

_____ **2.** attitude

_____ **3.** comment

a. a stated opinion made about someone or something

b. trust or depend on someone or something

c. an idea of how something is or how something should be done

d. the opinions and feelings that you usually have about someone or something

Use the academic words from the exercise above to complete the sentences.

4. We did not hear the _____ because the speaker's voice was too soft.

5. The teacher explained the _____ of supply-and-demand so that I could understand the idea.

6. Babies _____ their parents for all their needs.

7. Lina has a negative _____ toward spinach.

Complete the sentences with your own ideas.

Example: We have a good attitude about *moving to a new place* .

8. In my diary, I will write a comment about _____.

9. In science, I study the concept of _____.

10. We rely on rain for _____.

REMEMBER Many English words come from ancient Greek or Latin word parts, called roots. For example, the word *auto* is a Greek root meaning "self." An automatic machine is one that "works by itself." Knowing the meaning of common Greek and Latin roots can help you figure out the meanings of many English words.

Look at the chart below. Then add words from the box to the correct row on the chart.

| ~~asteroid~~ | dictator | pedal | pedestrian | podiatrist | podium | predict |

Root	Meaning	Origin	English Words
aster/astro	star	Greek	astronomical *asteroid* _____
pous/podos	foot	Greek	octopus **1.**_____ **2.**_____
ped/pedis	foot	Latin	centipede **3.**_____ **4.**_____
dict	say; speak	Latin	dictate **5.**_____ **6.**_____

Choose the word from the box below that best completes each sentence.

| ~~asteroid~~ | podiatrist | predict | pedestrian | podium |

Example: An _____*asteroid*_____ is a large object made of rock that moves about in space.

7. A doctor who takes care of people's feet is called a _____.

8. Fortune tellers try to _____, or say in advance, what will happen.

9. When you give a speech, you often stand at a tall narrow desk called a

    _____.

10. Someone who is walking instead of driving is called a _____.

READING STRATEGY | IDENTIFY MAIN IDEA AND DETAILS

Use with textbook page 179.

REMEMBER When you read, identify the main idea and details. The main idea is the most important idea in a passage. Details are small pieces of information that support the main idea.

Read each paragraph. Then answer the questions that follow.

The year is divided into seasons. Each season has its own type of weather. There are four seasons in a year. The seasons are spring, summer, fall, and winter. Each season lasts about three months.

1. What is the main idea of the passage above?

   _____

   _____

2. What are the details that support the main idea?

   _____

   _____

Using a homework planner is a great way to stay organized. Everytime you are in class, write down the homework in your homework planner. Then, when you are doing your homework, take out your planner. You will have all of your assignments neatly written down in one place.

3. What is the main idea of the passage above?

   _____

   _____

4. What are the details that support the main idea?

   _____

   _____

5. How can identifying the main idea and details help you to read with greater comprehension?

   _____

   _____

Choose the best answer for each item. Circle the letter of the correct answer.

1. The plover and the crocodile _____.

   a. help each other   **b.** ignore each other   **c.** harm each other

2. Owen is a hippo who became best friends with a _____.

   a. bird   **b.** wise man   **c.** tortoise

3. Owen was separated from his mother by a _____.

   a. group of hippos   **b.** tsunami   **c.** hunter

4. People took Owen to a(n) _____.

   a. coral reef   **b.** different ocean   **c.** animal shelter

5. The main idea of this article is that animals _____.

   a. are different from people   **b.** can become friends   **c.** are wild creatures

EXTENSION *Use with textbook page 185.*

Write the names of five animals in the chart below. Then research how these animals help people or other animals.

Animal	How the Animal Helps People or Other Animals
dogs	help blind people get around

GRAMMAR, USAGE, AND MECHANICS

Prepositions of Location *Use with textbook page 186.*

REMEMBER A preposition shows location or time. Some common prepositions of location are *under, below, in, behind, after, near, beneath, above, beside, between, on, across,* and *outside.*
Example: Please don't put the book on the table.

Complete each sentence with a word from the box.

behind	between	outside	below	on

1. He put a slice of cheese _____ two slices of bread to make a sandwich.

2. Europe lies _____ the Atlantic Ocean.

3. The roots of a tree lie _____ the ground.

4. The ducklings waddled _____ their mother, following her to the pond.

5. Inside the house it was quiet, but a great deal was going on _____ the window.

Write a sentence with the prepositional phrase in parentheses.

Example: (after another) *The students lined up one after another.*

6. (next to me)

_____

7. (beneath his name)

_____

8. (beside the chair)

_____

9. (in a suitcase)

_____

10. (on the roof)

_____

WRITING A PERSUASIVE PARAGRAPH

Write a Critical Evaluation *Use with textbook page 187.*

This is the outline that Tyler completed before writing his critical evaluation.

I. **Main Idea (introduce standards)** *Good students need to have certain traits.*
   A. *They need to be smart.*
   B. *They need to be dedicated, proud, and confident.*
   C. *They need to be willing to share what they know.*
II. **Main Idea (judge topic)** *Michaela is a student with these traits.*
   A. *She is very smart.*
   B. *She studies hard, takes pride in her work, and has a relaxed and friendly attitude.*

Complete your own outline for a critical evaluation of a person or issue.

I. **Main Idea (introduce standards)**

   A.

   B.

   C.

II. **Main Idea (judge topic)**

   A.

   B.

   C.

EDIT AND PROOFREAD   *Use with textbook page 194.*

Read the paragraph below carefully. Look for mistakes in spelling, punctuation, and grammar. Mark the mistakes with proofreader's marks (textbook page 454). Then rewrite the paragraph correctly on the lines below.

All students should wear uniforms to school and I have many good reasons for saying this. First, some schoolz have problems with kids being cruel to each other. They even form social groups to fashion. If everyone be wearing a uniform, everyone looks the same. Kids will get along better. Second, school uniforms increase school pride. Wearing a uniform sendz the message: "I belong to a special group of people in a special place." Students who feel they belong to their School community will work harder than those who feel cut off. The arguements in favor of school uniforms are strong. as a result, about one-quarter of america's public schools have a school uniform policy. Isnt' it time all schools put a school uniform policy into effect Yes!

_____

_____

_____

_____

_____

_____

_____

_____

_____

_____

Underline the vocabulary items you know and can use well. Review and practice any you haven't underlined. Underline them when you know them well.

Literary Words	Key Words	Academic Words	
dialect	assassinated	appropriate	attitude
mood	extraordinary	communicate	comment
suspense	founders	period	concept
figure of speech	resistance	precise	rely on
hyperbole	superintendent	achieve	
	tolerance	alter	
	arrangement	impact	
	cooperate	role	
	damage	consist	
	gigantic	establish	
	intruder	method	
	tsunami	stress	

Put a check by the skills you can perform well. Review and practice any you haven't checked off. Check them off when you can perform them well.

Skills	I can . . .
Word Study	☐ use apostrophes. ☐ recognize and spell words with silent *gh*. ☐ recognize and use synonyms and antonyms. ☐ recognize and use Greek and Latin roots.
Reading Strategies	☐ make inferences. ☐ identify problems and solutions. ☐ distinguish fact from opinion. ☐ identify main idea and details.
Grammar, Usage, and Mechanics	☐ write simple and compound sentences. ☐ use prepositions of time *in, on,* and *at* correctly. ☐ use placement of adjectives correctly. ☐ use prepositions of location correctly.
Writing	☐ write a book review. ☐ write using a question-and-answer format. ☐ write a diary entry. ☐ write a critical evaluation. ☐ write an expository essay.

Learn about Art with the Smithsonian
American Art Museum *Use with textbook pages 196–197.*

LEARNING TO LOOK

Look at *Mis Hermanos* by Jesse Treviño on page 196 in your textbook. Use a blank piece of paper to cover all of the men in the painting except the man on the far right, who is sitting on the fence and holding a glass. Write down four observations about the man on the far right who is holding a glass. State facts, not opinions.

Example: *He wears a watch on his right wrist.*

1. _____

2. _____

3. _____

4. _____

INTERPRETATION

Look at *Mis Hermanos* by Jesse Treviño again. Imagine that someone else joins the men in this painting.

Where should he or she be positioned in the painting?

Example: *He should be sitting on the fence on the right side.*

_____

_____

What should he or she wear?

_____

_____

Draw a simple sketch of the new person you would add to the painting.

Look at *Mis Hermanos* by Jesse Treviño again and *"Men exist for the sake of one another . . ."* by Jacob Lawrence on page 197 in your textbook. Write down three differences you see between the two artworks in the chart. Then write three similarities between them in the chart.

Jesse Treviño *Mis Hermanos*	Jacob Lawrence *"Men exist for the sake of one another . . ."*
Differences	
The men all have dark hair on their heads.	*The man has light hair on his head.*
1.	
2.	
3.	
Similarities	
4.	
5.	
6.	

Name _____ Date _____

What do we learn through winning and losing?

READING 1: "Soccer: The World Sport"

VOCABULARY **Key Words** *Use with textbook page 201.*

Write each word in the box next to its definition.

| athletes | boundaries | professional | responsibilities | sacrifice | uniforms |

Example: ___sacrifice___: to give something up

1. _____: outfits worn by members of a group, such as a sports team

2. _____: people who are good at sports

3. _____: things a person has a duty to do

4. _____: someone who gets paid to do something

5. _____: the lines that mark the edges of something, such as a playing field

Use the words in the box at the top of the page to complete the sentences.

6. I asked about the _____ of the job when I interviewed.

7. Even though I'm not a _____ artist, I love to draw.

8. She had to _____ a lot to become a skater, but it was worth it.

9. Our new _____ have our team logo.

10. _____ have to practice to be good at their sport.

Read the paragraph below. Pay attention to the underlined academic words.

The "Iditarod" is a famous, 1,161-mile dogsled race across Alaska. The cold weather and extreme length of the race require the racers and the dogs to be in their best physical shape. Good teamwork between man and dog is another important element of a successful dogsled team. The racers must focus on the dogs' performance and safety, and must project a positive attitude until the end. The event is considered one of the last great races of the world.

Write the academic words from the paragraph above next to their correct definitions.

Example: _____*require*_____: need something

1. _____: good or useful

2. _____: one part of a plan, system, piece of writing, and so on

3. _____: give all your attention to a particular person or thing

Use the academic words from the paragraph above to complete the sentences.

4. All his hard work had a _____ effect on his grades.

5. I know that if I _____ on the problem, I can figure it out.

6. Sports like soccer _____ a lot of practice.

7. Sports are an important _____ of my life.

Complete the sentences with your own ideas.

Example: Having a positive approach ___*can help you do well at things*___.

8. For me, sports and studying both require _____.

9. This year I will focus on _____.

10. The most interesting element of my current school project is

_____.

WORD STUDY Multiple-Meaning Words *Use with textbook page 203.*

> **REMEMBER** Some words in English have more than one meaning. For example, as a noun, *bat* refers to an animal or baseball equipment. As a verb, it means "to hit." Use context clues, the word's part of speech or a dictionary to determine which meaning is being used.

Read each sentence. Identify the part of speech of each underlined word. Then define the word. Check your work with a dictionary.

Sentence	Part of Speech	Meaning
I need to go to the store.	noun	a place that sells things
1. We took a break from studying.		
2. The pencil will break if you play with it.		
3. The spring on the bed is loose.		
4. Spring is my favorite season of all.		
5. Spring out of bed and get your chores done!		

Look at the sentences in the chart below. Write the meanings and part of speech of each word in the chart. Use a dictionary if needed.

Multiple-Meaning Word	Part of speech/Meaning	Part of speech/Meaning
We roast marshmallows over the fire. The boss will fire them.	noun: flames	verb: to remove from a job
6. The rose smelled so sweet. I rose from my chair in astonishment.		
7. Come to my place after school. Place the glass on the shelf, please.		
8. Gary pounds the post into the ground. The teacher will post the grades.		
9. We bought a tire for the car. The kids tire me out.		

REMEMBER When you read, it is important to check your understanding of the text you are reading. One good technique is to ask questions using the 5Ws: *Who?, Where?, When?, What?, Why?* Then try to answer the questions from what you've learned in the text.

Read the paragraph and answer the questions that follow.

Julio wanted to go to college. He studied hard. He went to an after-school math class because he found math difficult. At his high school outside Los Angeles, there are many athletic teams. Julio played on the tennis and water polo teams. After four years of hard work, Julio got into a great college.

1. Who is this passage about?

   _____

2. Where did this passage take place?

   _____

In 1872, my great-great grandparents left Italy. They travelled by boat to New York City. For many years, they struggled. My great-great grandfather worked as a lamplighter. My great-great grandmother worked as a maid. Life was hard.

3. Who is this passage about?

   _____

4. When do the events in this passage take place?

   _____

5. How do you think asking questions can help you to understand what you read better?

   _____

Name _____ Date _____

Choose the best answers for each item. Circle the letter of the correct answer.

1. Soccer is called "the simplest sport" because _____.

   a. it can only be played in the summer
   b. it requires very little equipment
   c. it doesn't have any official rules

2. Except for the goalie, soccer players can't use their _____.

   a. hands
   b. feet
   c. heads

3. The biggest event in soccer is the _____.

   a. Wimbledon Championship
   b. Super Bowl
   c. World Cup

4. In the United States, soccer is _____.

   a. the most popular sport in the entire country
   b. the fastest-growing team sport
   c. not very popular

5. One special thing about the Fugees team is that _____.

   a. the players are all children of famous players
   b. the players all come from war-torn countries
   c. the players are all members of a famous rock band

EXTENSION   *Use with textbook page 211.*

In the United States, two kinds of football are played: American football and soccer. Research to find information about both games. Then use the information to complete the chart below.

	American Football	**Soccer**
Number of players on the field	11	11
6. Shape of ball		
7. Term for field		
8. Length of game (time)		
9. Name and length of game divisions (time)		
10. Distance between goalposts		

GRAMMAR, USAGE, AND MECHANICS

Present Perfect *Use with textbook page 212.*

> **REMEMBER** Use the present perfect to describe actions that happened at an unspecified time in the past. Form the present perfect with *has* or *have* + the past participle of a verb. Use *has* with a singular subject and *have* with a plural subject.
> **Example:** The fans have arrived early.
> Also use the present perfect with *for* or *since* to describe actions that began in the past and continue into the present.
> **Examples:** We have worn these soccer uniforms for a year (and we are still wearing them). Since the beginning of the season, we have won three games (and we will win more before the end of the season). Finally, use the present perfect with *ever* in questions asking whether someone has done something "at any time in the past" or "in his or her entire life."
> **Example:** *Have* you ever seen a soccer game?

Complete each sentence below with the verb in parentheses. Write each verb in the present perfect.

Example: (call) Fans ___*have called*___ him the greatest soccer player.

1. (elect) They _____ her to the Soccer Hall of Fame.

2. (organize) Our school _____ a soccer team.

3. (play) Since 1984, professional soccer players _____ in the Olympic Games.

4. (practice) She _____ for hours.

5. (win) _____ your team ever

   _____ a game?

Write sentences that use the present perfect of the verbs in parentheses.

Example: (start) ___*We have started a soccer team.*___

6. (need) _____

7. (watch) _____

8. (focus) _____

9. (require) _____

10. (share) _____

WRITING AN EXPOSITORY PARAGRAPH

Write a Newspaper Article *Use with textbook page 213.*

This is the 5Ws chart that Anna completed before writing her newspaper article.

Who?	*soccer players from 32 countries*
Where?	*Germany*
When?	*June 9 to July 9, 2006*
What?	*FIFA World Cup soccer tournament*
Why?	*To compete to be the world champions*

Complete your own 5Ws chart for a newspaper article about a sports event or other competition or game that you found exciting.

Who?	
Where?	
When?	
What?	
Why?	

UNIT 4

What do we learn through winning and losing?

READING 2: "Casey at the Bat" / "Swift Things Are Beautiful" / "Buffalo Dusk"

VOCABULARY **Literary Words** *Use with textbook page 215.*

REMEMBER Poetry often uses patterns to create effects. The regular, repeated pattern of sounds is called **rhythm**. Repeating the same sound is **repetition**. The pattern made by words that end with the same sound is the **rhyme scheme**.

Read each sentence in the chart. Underline the words you stress as you read. Then check the box to show if the sentence uses rhyme, rhythm, or repetition.

Sentence	Rhythm	Repetition	Rhyme
Don't be <u>late</u>, <u>Nate</u>, for our <u>skate</u>.			✔
1. We will run, run, run down the road.			
2. Will they stay, or go away, and come back another day?			
3. Look left, look right, look left again.			
4. I say I do not hope, but I do hope, I hope with all my heart.			
5. Our faces will glow as we race through the snow.			

Read the nursery rhyme "Humpty Dumpty." Circle examples of repetition. Underline the words that rhyme. Then use the letters *a*, *b*, and *c* to label the rhyme scheme.

Humpty Dumpty

Example: (Humpty Dumpty) sat on a <u>wall</u>. ___*a*___

6. Humpty Dumpty had a great fall. _____

7. All the king's horses _____

8. And all the king's men _____

9. Couldn't put Humpty together again _____

10. Does this poem have rhythm? _____

VOCABULARY **Academic Words** *Use with textbook page 216.*

Read the paragraph below. Pay attention to the underlined academic words.

> The poem "Casey at the Bat" is about a baseball game. It is thirteen stanzas long, so it is not a <u>brief</u> poem. Each stanza has a definite <u>structure</u>—each is four lines long. Every two lines rhyme with each other, and this poetic <u>device</u> helps create rhythm. The poet describes the game using colorful language. For example, he calls a baseball a "leather-covered <u>sphere</u>." He captures the spirit of the fans as they loudly <u>respond</u> to the game. The suspense builds as the game goes on, so that the reader really wonders what is going to happen in the <u>final</u> stanza.

Write the letter of the correct definition next to each word.

Example: ___c___ brief   **a.** last in a series of actions, events, or parts of something

_____ **1.** device   **b.** the way in which the parts of something connect with each other to form a whole

_____ **2.** final   **c.** continuing for a short time

_____ **3.** respond   **d.** something in the shape of a ball

_____ **4.** sphere   **e.** react to something that has been said or done

_____ **5.** structure   **f.** a way of achieving a particular purpose

Use the academic words from the exercise above to complete the sentences.

6. An orange is an example of a _____.

7. He asked a question and waited for me to _____.

8. Honeycombs have a _____ of six-sided cells.

Complete the sentences with your own ideas.

Example: One example of a literary device is *alliteration, or words that start with the same sound.*

9. When my homework takes a brief amount of time, I _____.

10. The final thing I do at the end of each day is _____.

Use with textbook page 217.

> **REMEMBER** The long /ī/ can be spelled in many ways, including *i* as in *grind*, *i_e* as in *spike*, *y* as in *fry*, *igh* as in *bright*, and *ie* as in *lie*. Knowing these patterns can help you spell and say many words with the long /ī/ correctly.

Read the words in the box below. Then write each word in the correct column in the chart.

pint	fried	flight	fly	bike
type	precise	denied	why	delight
behind	pie	find	bribe	night

/ī/ spelled *i*	/ī/ spelled *i_e*	/ī/ spelled *y*	/ī/ spelled *igh*	/ī/ spelled *ie*
pint				

Write the correct spelling pattern for /ī/ in each word below.

Example: bride _____ */ī/ spelled i_e* _____

1. mind _____

2. dry _____

3. might _____

4. tied _____

5. divide _____

6. sign _____

READING STRATEGY | **READ FOR ENJOYMENT** *Use with textbook page 217.*

REMEMBER When you read for enjoyment, you aren't just reading for information. You are reading to be entertained by other things, such as the characters, the setting, or the words.

Read and answer the questions below.

1. What is your favorite book?

_____

2. What made the book so enjoyable?

_____

_____

_____

3. What is the name of your all-time favorite character in a book?

_____

4. What did you like best about that character?

_____

_____

_____

5. Which kinds of texts do you most enjoy reading? Why?

_____

_____

_____

_____

_____

_____

_____

Choose the best answer for each item. Circle the letter of the correct answer.

1. Why does the narrator say that the outlook wasn't brilliant for the Mudville team?

   a. one of the players died during the game

   b. they were losing

   c. they were winning

2. The team's fans want _____.

   a. the game to go into overtime

   b. Flynn to get up to bat

   c. Casey to get up to bat

3. At the end of "Casey at the Bat," the people in the town are sad because _____.

   a. Casey did not get to play

   b. Casey hit a home run

   c. Casey struck out

4. In the poem "Swift Things Are Beautiful," the swift things named include _____.

   a. lightning and wind

   b. cats and waterfalls

   c. skaters and swimmers

5. In "Buffalo Dusk," the poet describes buffaloes on the _____.

   a. mountains

   b. prairie

   c. seashore

RESPONSE TO LITERATURE *Use with textbook page 225.*

In this section you read three poems: "Casey at the Bat," "Swift Things Are Beautiful," and "Buffalo Dusk." Research to find another poem that you like. Copy the poem in the space below. Remember to include the title of the poem and the name of the poet.

GRAMMAR, USAGE, AND MECHANICS

Simple Past: More Irregular Verbs *Use with textbook page 226.*

> **REMEMBER** Use the simple past to talk about actions that were completed in the past or to talk about conditions that happened at a specific time in the past. You must memorize the simple past form of irregular verbs.

Complete each sentence with the simple past of the verb in parentheses.

Example: (read) When I was little, my mother _____*read*_____ a poem to me every night.

1. (write) Ernest Lawrence Thayer _____ a poem about baseball.

2. (hit) Casey was the player who _____ the ball.

3. (stand) He _____ at the mound.

4. (begin) We _____ to like poetry after hearing the reading.

5. (understand) We _____ the rhyme scheme.

Read each question below. Notice the underlined verb in each question. Complete the answers to each question by writing the verb in the simple past.

Example: What did you <u>think</u> of the poem?

   I thought the poem was funny. _____

6. How many dishes did the waiter <u>break</u>?

   The waiter _____ twelve dishes.

7. Did the candidate <u>shake</u> everyone's hand?

   Yes, the candidate _____ everyone's hand.

8. Where did the woman <u>keep</u> her important papers?

   The woman _____ her important papers in her desk.

9. When did the soccer player <u>become</u> famous?

   The soccer player _____ famous in 1997.

10. How many times did the pitcher <u>throw</u> the ball?

   The pitcher _____ the ball five times.

WRITING AN EXPOSITORY PARAGRAPH

Write a Response to Literature *Use with textbook page 227.*

This is the word web that Andrew completed before writing his paragraph.

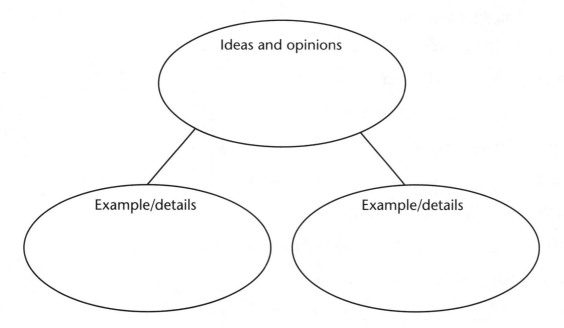

Ideas and opinions

"Buffalo Dusk" is a peaceful, yet very upsetting poem.

Example/details

Buffaloes once roamed free.

Example/details

Both the buffaloes and "those who saw the buffaloes" are gone.

Complete your own word web for a response to the poem "Casey at the Bat."

Ideas and opinions

Example/details

Example/details

UNIT 4

What do we learn through winning and losing?

READING 3: "The Hare and the Tortoise" / "Orpheus and Eurydice"

VOCABULARY **Literary Words** *Use with textbook page 229.*

REMEMBER A **fable** is a short story that has a **moral**, or lesson. Fables often include **personification**, or animal characters that talk and act like human beings. A **myth** is a story from long ago; myths often try to explain events in nature, such as the seasons of the year.

Label each description as myth, fable, moral, or personification.

Description	Myth, Fable, Moral, or Personification?
A story that explains the origin of the seasons of the year	*myth*
1. Don't count your chickens before they've hatched.	
2. A story about an ant and a grasshopper that teaches a lesson	
3. A grateful lion	

Read the following story. Then answer the questions that follow.

A crow was very thirsty. When he saw a jug of water in a garden, he leaned in to take a drink. He soon realized that the jug was too narrow. Finally, he had an idea. He picked up pebbles with his beak and dropped them into the jug. Soon, the water rose higher. At last, the thirsty crow was able to drink. This shows that necessity is the mother of invention.

4. Is this story a fable or a myth? _____

5. What is one example of an animal behaving like a human being in the story?

_____

_____

Read the paragraph below. Pay attention to the underlined academic words.

Our teacher said she would <u>instruct</u> the class on how to make a glossary. Her <u>objective</u>, she said, was for us to learn the new vocabulary terms. She told us to <u>define</u> each vocabulary word and write a sentence including it. Then she asked us to draw a picture that would help us remember each word. She said the picture could be in any <u>style</u> we wanted—simple, complicated, or even comical. I think the glossary is a great idea.

Write the academic words from the paragraph above next to their correct definitions.

Example: _____*style*_____ : a way of doing, making, or painting something that is typical of a particular period

1. _____ : teach someone or show him or her how to do something

2. _____ : something that you are working hard to achieve

3. _____ : show or describe what something is or means

Use academic words from the paragraph above to complete the sentences.

4. My favorite _____ of painting is Impressionism, which was popular in the late 1800s.

5. You need to understand something very well to _____ someone else on the subject.

6. Sometimes you can use clues in a sentence to _____ a word you don't know.

7. It helps to have a clear _____ before starting something.

Complete the sentences with your own ideas.

Example: It can be easier to define a word if *it is similar to another word you know* .

8. I could instruct someone to _____ .

9. My style of writing is _____ .

10. My objective for school this year is _____ .

WORD STUDY Spellings for *r*-Controlled Vowels

Use with textbook page 231.

> **REMEMBER** When *r* comes after a vowel, the vowel stands for a special sound—the *r*-controlled vowel. The *r*-controlled vowel sound can be spelled *ar* as in *far*, *er* as in *stern*, *ir* as in *bird*, *or* as in *orchard*, and *ur* as in *burn*.

Read the words in the box below. Then write each word in the correct column in the chart.

chart	force	thirst	father	fur
part	horn	turf	fern	stir

/är/ as in *bar*	/ər/ as in *concern*	/ər/ as in *flirt*	/ôr/ as in *nor*	/ər/ as in *surf*
chart				

Write the *r*-controlled vowel in each below.

Example: hurt _____*ur*_____

1. spark _____

2. mother _____

3. remorse _____

4. sir _____

5. embark _____

6. forth _____

> **REMEMBER** When you read, try to identify the author's purpose, or the reason the author wrote the text. The main purposes an author has to write are: to entertain, to inform, or to persuade.

Read each passage below. Then answer the questions that follow each passage.

Animal shelters are a great place to find a pet. My cousin Jack adopted a mutt he called Sparky from an animal shelter. Sparky was shy at first, but soon he got used to all the love and attention he got from Jack. Then, one night, a fire started in the basement. Jack was fast asleep, but Sparky barked and barked. When Jack still didn't get up Sparky gave his hand a gentle nip. Jack woke up. Sparky saved him!

1. What is the author's purpose for writing?

_____

2. What clues in the text indicate the author's purpose for writing?

_____

Do you feel tired and have low energy in the morning? There's something easy that can help. It's called breakfast. Breakfast will give you energy and make you feel healthy. You may not like eggs, oatmeal, or cereal for breakfast, but there are other healthy choices, too. You could have yogurt and fruit. You could have peanut butter on toast or a ham sandwich. You could even eat leftover pizza.

3. What is the author's purpose for writing?

_____

4. How does the author show his or her purpose?

_____

5. How can the strategy of identifying an author's purpose help you to understand a text better?

_____

_____

COMPREHENSION   *Use with textbook page 236.*

Choose the best answer for each item. Circle the letter of the correct answer.

1. In the story "The Hare and the Tortoise," Hare loses the race because he _____.

   a. falls asleep   **b.** loses his way   **c.** forgets about
                                                                       the race

2. The moral of "The Hare and the Tortoise" is "Slow and steady . . . " _____.

   a. always ready   **b.** wins the race   **c.** nice and easy

3. In "Orpheus and Eurydice," Orpheus is a _____.

   a. famous writer   **b.** skilled carpenter   **c.** talented musician

4. To rescue his wife, Orpheus travels to _____.

   a. the Underworld   **b.** the Mediterranean Sea   **c.** the top of Mount
                                                                               Olympus

5. Orpheus loses his wife again when he _____.

   a. fails to charm   **b.** breaks his lyre   **c.** looks back too soon
       Hades

RESPONSE TO LITERATURE   *Use with textbook page 237.*

The story "Orpheus and Eurydice" reflects the time when it was first told. Orpheus plays a lyre, and Eurydice dies when she is bitten by a snake. Imagine how a story like this might be told today. What kind of music might Orpheus play? How might Eurydice die? What would their names be? Use your imagination to complete the graphic organizer for a modern retelling of the story.

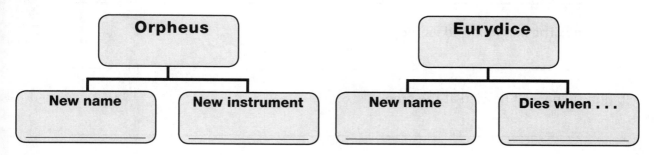

GRAMMAR, USAGE, AND MECHANICS

Adverbs with -ly *Use with textbook page 238.*

REMEMBER An adverb usually describes the action of a verb. For example, it can tell how an action happened. An adverb can appear at the beginning, middle, or end of a sentence. An adverb can also appear before or after the verb. Many adverbs are formed by adding *-ly* to an adjective. Do not confuse adverbs that end in *-ly* with adjectives that end in *-y* (such as *pretty* and *rainy*).

Complete the chart by forming an adverb from each adjective.

Adjective	Adverb
1. sad	
2. bold	
3. final	
4. beautiful	
5. passionate	

Turn the adjectives in parentheses into adverbs. Then rewrite each sentence, inserting the adverbs where shown by the caret (ʌ).

Example: (soft) The lion crept ʌ through the high grass.

   The lion crept softly through the high grass.

6. (clear) We saw the wolf ʌ in the moonlight.

_____

7. (bright) The moon shone ʌ in the night sky.

_____

8. (careful) The lion ʌ followed its prey.

_____

9. (loud) The wolf howled ʌ at the moon.

_____

10. (recent) The rabbit had ʌ won a race.

_____

Name _____ Date _____

Write to Compare and Contrast *Use with textbook page 239.*

This is the Venn diagram that Wendy completed before writing her paragraphs.

Topic A *"The Hare and the Tortoise"*   Topic B *"Orpheus and Eurydice"*

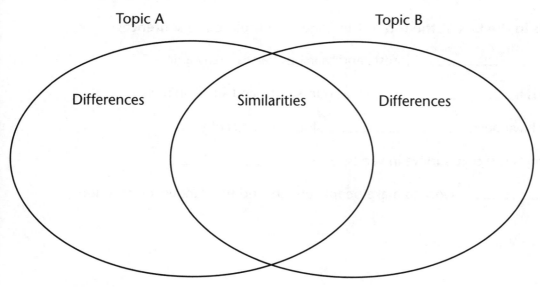

Differences
*fable with a moral
Hare can still live
happily ever after.*

Similarities
*ancient Greek stories
two main characters
One character acts
without thinking and
suffers a loss.*

Differences
*how-and-why myth
Orpheus stays sad
for the rest of his
life.*

Complete your own Venn diagram for two paragraphs that compare and contrast two people, places, or things.

Topic A   Topic B

Differences   Similarities   Differences

What do we learn through winning and losing?

READING 4: "Going, Going, Gone?" /
"Ivory-Billed Woodpeckers Make Noise"

VOCABULARY **Key Words** *Use with textbook page 241.*

Write each word in the box next to its definition.

| conservationists | destruction | extinct | habitats | ornithology | predator |

Example: __ornithology__: the study of birds

1. _____: people who work to save natural things

2. _____: the process of destroying something

3. _____: places where plants or animals naturally live

4. _____: an animal that kills and eats other animals

5. _____: no longer existing

Use the words in the box at the top of the page to complete the sentences.

6. The _____ of forests and marshes harms many animals.

7. The hawk is a _____ that hunts birds and small animals.

8. Dinosaurs have been _____ for thousands of years.

9. Some animals can only survive in very specific _____.

10. _____ work to make people understand the dangers of pollution.

VOCABULARY Academic Words *Use with textbook page 242.*

Read the paragraph below. Pay attention to the underlined academic words.

Many plants and animals are disappearing from our planet. <u>Statistics</u> show that about 11,000 animals and plants are nearing total extinction. Scientists can only <u>estimate</u> how many more species are endangered. Climate change, pollution, and disease are some of the <u>factors</u> that can lead a species to disappear. Taking care of the <u>environment</u> is one way people can help save plants and animals from extinction.

Write the letter of the correct definition next to each word.

Example: ___c___ environment

_____ 1. estimate

_____ 2. factors

_____ 3. statistics

a. a collection of numbers that represents facts or measurements

b. several things that influence or cause a situation

c. the land, water, and air in which people, animals, and plants live

d. judge the value or size of something

Use the academic words from the exercise above to above complete the sentences.

4. You can _____ how many jellybeans are in the jar.

5. Many different _____ led to the team's success.

6. Some plants need a lot of water, but some can live in a dry _____.

7. They tried to memorize the _____ for each player on the other team.

Complete the sentences with your own ideas.

Example: The environment where penguins live is ___*very cold*_____.

8. Some factors that can affect my decisions are _____.

9. To estimate the size of my room, I should _____.

10. I use statistics to _____.

REMEMBER Homophones are words that sound the same but have different meanings and spellings. For example, *tern* and *turn* are homophones. A *ring* is a circle; *wring* means "to twist." To decide which homophone to use, first see how the word is spelled. If you are still confused, use a dictionary.

Write the definitions for each pair of homophones in the chart. Use a dictionary if needed.

Words	Definitions
guest; guessed	*visitor; supposed*
1. hall; haul	
2. racquet; racket	
3. flour; flower	
4. gorilla; guerilla	
5. heard; herd	

Write the definitions for each pair of homophones. Then use the words in one or two sentences that show their meaning.

Example: heel; heal ___*back part of the foot; cure*___
___*The cut on her heel will heal in a week.*___

6. aunt; ant _____

_____

7. they're; their _____

_____

8. threw; through _____

_____

9. Jim; gym _____

_____

10. sail; sale _____

_____

READING STRATEGY | RECOGNIZE CAUSE AND EFFECT

Use with textbook page 243.

> **REMEMBER** When you recognize cause and effect, you understand the effect (what happened) and the cause (why it happened). Look for events, reasons, and clue words such as *so, because, because of, therefore,* and *as a result.*

Read each passage. Then answer the questions that follow.

"Here—you can have the last piece of pie," said Omar.
"But you love pumpkin pie," said Reem. "Why are you being so nice?"
"I just appreciate having a nice big sister like you."
"There has to be more than that."
"Well, okay. I accidentally knocked your tennis trophies off the shelf and broke one."

1. What was the cause in this passage?

   _____

2. What was the effect in this passage?

   _____

"I've got it!" said Professor Okumbo. She swirled the test tube and looked at the blue liquid in it. "From now on, no one will ever get sneezes, sniffles, or watery eyes. I've cured the common cold!" Pretty soon, Dr. Okumbo's cold fighting syrup was sold in drugstores all over the country. As a result, she became rich. Nobody ever suffered from a cold again.

3. What was the cause in this passage?

   _____

4. What were the effects in this passage?

   _____

5. How can the strategy of recognizing causes and effects help you to understand what you read better?

   _____

Choose the best answer for each item. Circle the letter of the correct answer.

1. "Going, Going, Gone?" says that the main cause of bird species becoming extinct

   is _____.

   a. disease   **b.** natural disasters   **c.** humans

2. In "Going, Going, Gone?" bird experts were excited by a possible sighting of _____.

   a. three passenger   **b.** a Carolina parakeet   **c.** an ivory-billed
   pigeons   woodpecker

3. In modern times, the first bird wiped out by humans was _____.

   a. the Carolina parakeet   **b.** the dodo   **c.** the passenger pigeon

4. The only parrot native to the eastern United States was the _____.

   a. passenger pigeon   **b.** ivory-billed woodpecker   **c.** Carolina parakeet

5. Conservationists in Arkansas are trying to _____.

   a. help woodpeckers   **b.** kill woodpeckers   **c.** stop tree-cutting

EXTENSION *Use with textbook page 249.*

The reading "Going, Going, Gone?" talks about bird species that are in danger or have become extinct. Birds aren't the only animals that are in danger. Research five more animals that are in danger or have already become extinct. Use the information you find to complete the table below.

Animal	Habitat	At Risk Because . . .
Giant Panda	high, cold forests in China	hunting by humans; habitat being destroyed by humans

GRAMMAR, USAGE, AND MECHANICS

Showing Cause and Effect: *because, because of,* and *so*

Use with textbook page 250.

> **REMEMBER** Writers signal cause and effect with expressions such as *because, because of,* and *so. Because* and *so* are used in independent clauses. An independent clause is a complete sentence. It contains a subject and a verb, and it expresses a complete thought. Notice that there is no comma before *because* when it introduces an independent clause. There is a comma before *so,* however.
> **Examples:** He did well on the test because he studied hard. It is a sunny day, *so* we are going to the beach.
> The phrase *because of* must be followed by a noun or a noun phrase.
> **Example:** We did not go to the beach because of the rain.

Complete each sentence below with *because, so,* or *because of.*

Example: I am tired _____*because*_____ I am studying hard.

1. He was happy _____ it was a beautiful day.

2. It might rain later, _____ I will carry an umbrella.

3. The team won the game _____ the players cooperated.

4. The team won the game _____ the players' cooperation.

5. We are celebrating my grandfather's birthday tomorrow,

   _____ I am helping to clean the house.

Finish each sentence by describing a cause or an effect. Use the word or phrase in parentheses.

Example: (because) She became a doctor ___*because she wanted to help people.*___

6. (because) He has a lot of friends _____

7. (so) The math test will be hard, _____

8. (because) She closed the window _____

9. (so) It was a beautiful day, _____

10. (because of) There will be no school on Monday _____

WRITING AN EXPOSITORY PARAGRAPH

Write a Cause-and-Effect Explanation *Use with textbook page 251.*

This is the cause-and-effect chart that Tamar completed before writing her paragraph.

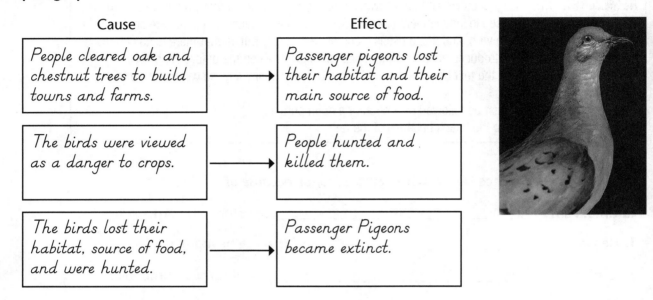

Cause

People cleared oak and chestnut trees to build towns and farms.

The birds were viewed as a danger to crops.

The birds lost their habitat, source of food, and were hunted.

Effect

Passenger pigeons lost their habitat and their main source of food.

People hunted and killed them.

Passenger Pigeons became extinct.

Complete your own cause-and-effect chart for a paragraph that gives reasons why the ivory-billed woodpecker was nearly wiped out.

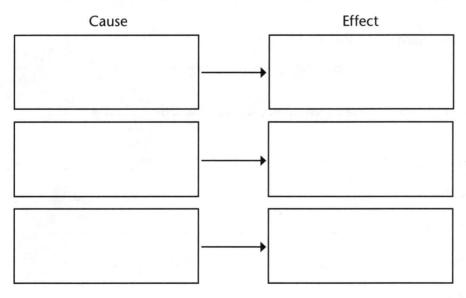

Cause

Effect

EDIT AND PROOFREAD   *Use with textbook page 258.*

Read the paragraph below carefully. Look for mistakes in spelling, punctuation, and grammar. Mark the mistakes with proofreader's marks (textbook page 454). Then rewrite the paragraph correctly on the lines below.

Last week we went on a whale watch. We had a list of things to bring: sunscreen, sunglasses, warm cloths, and sneakers. We brought our cameras, two. As we left the harbor a seal popped up and circled around our boat for a few minutes. As we went farther out to see we saw different kinds of whales One whale come very close to the boat. The captain, turned off the engines as the whale swam around the boat. it was amazing to see a whale so close! We also saw lots of birds. When Whales are feeding, seagulls and other birds pick up the scraps they leave behined. One gull landed right on a whale's head! I didnt want the day to end.

_____

_____

_____

_____

_____

_____

_____

_____

_____

Underline the vocabulary items you know and can use well. Review and practice any you haven't underlined. Underline them when you know them well.

Literary Words	Key Words	Academic Words	
rhythm	athletes	element	define
repetition	boundaries	focus	instruct
rhyme scheme	professional	positive	objective
fable	responsibilities	require	style
moral	sacrifice	brief	environment
personification	uniforms	device	estimate
myth	conservationists	final	factors
	destruction	respond	statistics
	extinct	sphere	
	habitats	structure	
	ornithology		
	predator		

Put a check by the skills you can perform well. Review and practice any you haven't checked off. Check them off when you can perform them well.

Skills	I can . . .
Word Study	☐ recognize words with multiple meanings. ☐ recognize and spell words with the long vowel sound /ī/. ☐ recognize and spell *r*-controlled vowels. ☐ recognize and spell homophones.
Reading Strategies	☐ ask questions. ☐ read for enjoyment. ☐ identify the author's purpose. ☐ recognize cause and effect.
Grammar, Usage, and Mechanics	☐ use the present perfect. ☐ use the simple past of irregular verbs. ☐ use adverbs with -*ly*. ☐ use expressions showing cause and effect.
Writing	☐ write a newspaper article. ☐ write a response to literature. ☐ write to compare and contrast. ☐ write a cause-and-effect explanation. ☐ write an expository essay.

Learn about Art with the Smithsonian
American Art Museum *Use with textbook pages 260–261.*

LEARNING TO LOOK

Look at *Baseball at Night* by Morris Kantor on page 261 in your textbook. How many shapes can you find in the painting? List them below.

Example: _____*The pitcher stands in a circle.*_____

_____

_____

_____

_____

INTERPRETATION

Look at *Rejects from the Bat Factory* by Mark Sfirri on page 260 of your textbook. The artist created five different bat shapes out of five different woods. Which is your favorite? Why?

_____

_____

If you could add a bat to this work of art what would it look like? Sketch it below.

What material would it be made from?

_____

_____

Where would you place it? Why?

_____

_____

Look at *Baseball at Night* again. Imagine you could interview a fan in the stands. What would you ask him or her? Use *Who, Where, When, What, Why* and *How* to frame your questions.

Example: How _*often do you come to the night games?*_

1. Who _____

   _____

2. Where _____

   _____

3. When _____

   _____

4. What _____

   _____

5. Why _____

   _____

6. How _____

   _____

UNIT 5

How are courage and imagination linked?

READING 1: From *The Secret Garden*

VOCABULARY **Literary Words** *Use with textbook page 265.*

> **REMEMBER** Playwrights start by **setting the scene**, or giving details about the time and place. The **list of characters** shows each person in the play. The **stage directions** tell actors how to look and act. Stage directions also tell about the scenery and costumes.

Read each passage. In the space provided, write *setting the scene* if the passage gives facts about the time and place. Write *character* if the passage describes a character. Write *stage directions* if the passage tells the actors and set designers what to do.

Literary Word	Example
character	Cynthia Jones, an Asian factory worker, age twenty
1.	Around 2005. A kitchen in a country house.
2.	Nick Jameson, an artist, age thirty-three
3.	[*Luis shakes Nita's hand while the lights dim.*]
4.	World War II. Chicago's Southside. Living room of a small apartment. Young child sleeping on the sofa.
5.	[*Nita exits the stage. A spotlight shines on a table in the center of the stage.*]

Read the passage from the play "Moving Day." Write *setting, character,* or *stage direction* in the circles. The first example is done.

Moving Day

Characters

6. Mama, strong woman but very tired — *character*

Noelle Richards, age 15

7. Present day. Living room of a big house. Lots of boxes stacked up.

Mama: [*Sighing and looking at her watch*] This is not going well. Not at all. **9.**

8. Noelle: [*Smiling at her mother*] How can I help?

Mama: [*Laughing*] I wish I knew! Look at this mess! **10.**

Read the paragraph below. Pay attention to the underlined academic words.

> My school is putting on the <u>drama</u> *Our Town* this year. The director is very good. He is teaching the actors how to <u>convey</u> emotion through voice, movement, and expression. He is working to make sure everyone on stage and behind the scenes will <u>cooperate</u>. He is also always very helpful when I <u>approach</u> him with a question or problem.

Write the academic words from the paragraph above next to their correct definitions.

Example: _____*drama*_____: a play for the theater, television, radio, and so forth

1. _____: work with someone else to achieve something that you both want

2. _____: communicate a message or information, with or without using words

3. _____: move closer to someone or something

Use the academic words from the paragraph above to complete the sentences.

4. The _____ was performed first on the stage and then on television.

5. Lisa and her parents _____ to get their chores done faster.

6. You should never _____ a strange dog; stay far away!

7. Actors _____ feelings with their faces, voices, and body movements.

Complete the sentences with your own ideas.

Example: In our class drama, I'm hoping _____*to get the lead part*_____.

8. It is important to cooperate because _____.

9. You should never approach a bear because _____.

10. Dogs convey they are happy by _____.

WORD STUDY **Spelling Words with *oo*** *Use with textbook page 267.*

REMEMBER The letters *oo* can stand for either the short sound /o͝o/ as in *look* or the long sound /o͞o/ as in *moose*. Knowing these sound spellings helps you spell and say many words correctly.

Read the words in the box below to yourself. Listen for the long or short sound of *oo*. Then write each word in the correct column in the chart.

~~rookie~~	school	brook	snooze	spoon
misunderstood	root	pocketbook	balloon	foot

short sound of *oo* as in *cook*	long sound of *oo* as in *shampoo*
rookie	

Read each word below to yourself, listening for the long or short sound of *oo*. Write *long oo* or *short oo* next to each word. Then think of a word that rhymes with each word and has the same sound spelling. Write the word and use the rhyming words in a sentence of your own.

Examples: monsoon *long oo   balloon   I lost my balloon during the monsoon.*

foot *short oo   soot   How did only one foot get covered with soot?*

1. pool _____

2. scoot _____

3. crook _____

4. goose _____

5. wood _____

Use with textbook page 267.

> **REMEMBER** Analyzing text structure helps you to understand what kind of text you are reading. Different kinds of writing have different kinds of text structure. For instance, stories are written in sentences and paragraphs, while poems are usually written in stanzas. Plays are made up mostly of dialogue.

Read each passage and answer the questions that follow.

> A day in the sun
> is a whole lot of fun
> we skip and play
> the lovely day away!

1. What are some features of the text above that show it is a poem?

   _____

   _____

2. What are some ways the text structure of a poem is different than the text structure of a story?

   _____

   _____

> JAMIE: Did you do your homework?
> JOHN: Yes. I always do my homework.
> JAMIE: So do I.
> JOHN: Great! Let's go and play.

3. What is the text structure of the passage above?

   _____

4. What features in the text helped you to understand that the text is a play?

   _____

   _____

5. How can the strategy of analyzing text structure help you to understand what you read?

   _____

COMPREHENSION   *Use with textbook page 276.*

Choose the best answer for each item. Circle the letter of the correct answer.

1. Dickon is not like most kids because he _____.

   a. talks to animals   **b.** comes from India   **c.** likes gardens

2. Mrs. Craven's favorite place was _____.

   a. her room   **b.** the garden   **c.** the big house

3. The children _____.

   a. ignore the garden   **b.** dislike the garden   **c.** fix the garden

4. The end of the play suggests that _____.

   a. Mr. Craven will   **b.** Colin will leave   **c.** Mary will marry
      be happier   Dickon

5. This play shows the importance and power of _____.

   a. animals   **b.** opening gardens   **c.** friendship and love
                                  to everyone

RESPONSE to LITERATURE   *Use with textbook page 277.*

Write a scene that tells what happens next in the play. Set the scene and use stage directions. Write at least five lines.

_____

_____

_____

_____

_____

_____

_____

_____

GRAMMAR, USAGE, AND MECHANICS

More Adverbs with -ly *Use with textbook page 278.*

> **REMEMBER** An adverb is the part of speech that gives more information about an action. It describes how an action is performed. **Example:** The actor spoke quietly.
> Most adverbs can be recognized easily by their -ly ending.

Complete each sentence by forming an adverb from the adjective in parentheses.

Example: (perfect) The father had found a present that suited his daughter _____*perfectly*_____.

1. (excited) On the morning of her birthday she _____ opened her present.

2. (loving) Her father was watching her _____.

3. (careful) She _____ pulled off layer after layer of wrapping paper.

4. (happy) When she saw what was inside, she clapped her hands _____.

5. (clear) She _____ loved the present.

Write your own sentences describing an action by using the adverb of the adjective listed.

Example: slow ___*The runner runs slowly up the hill.*___

6. angry _____

_____

7. bold _____

_____

8. correct _____

_____

9. creative _____

_____

10. thoughtful _____

_____

WRITING AN EXPOSITORY PARAGRAPH

Write a Formal E-mail *Use with textbook page 279.*

This is the problem-solution chart that Angelina completed before writing her e-mail.

Problem	Solution
The bare surroundings of the monument in Law Park don't express its importance.	Start a community garden to make a beautiful setting for the monument.

Complete your own problem-solution chart for a formal e-mail to your community's mayor about a problem you want to solve in your neighborhood.

Problem	Solution

VOCABULARY **Key Words** *Use with textbook page 281.*

Write each word in the box next to its definition.

| anniversary | atomic bomb | canvases | chaos | inspiration | mural |

Example: _____*mural*_____: a painting that is painted on a wall

1. _____: strong, heavy pieces of cloth that are used for making paintings

2. _____: something that encourages you to do something good

3. _____: a situation in which everything is confused

4. _____: a date on which something important happened in an earlier year

5. _____: a very powerful bomb that splits atoms to cause an extremely large explosion

Use the words in the box at the top of the page to complete the sentences.

6. The _____ is the most powerful weapon in the world today.

7. The class painted a _____ that covered an entire wall!

8. The artist made her own _____ by stretching the heavy fabric on wood frames.

9. The artist got her _____ for the painting from nature.

10. The fire drill in the middle of the test caused great _____.

VOCABULARY Academic Words *Use with textbook page 282.*

Read the paragraph below. Pay attention to the underlined academic words.

> My brother and his wife decided to <u>construct</u> a new home in Vail, Colorado. They chose to live in a <u>region</u> with snow and mountains because they like to ski. I couldn't help but <u>react</u> with excitement when I heard about their new home. I love to ski, too! When the <u>circumstances</u> are right, I'll ask if I can come for a visit.

Write the letter of the correct definition next to each word.

Example: ___c___ region

     a. the facts or conditions that affect a situation, action, or event

_____ **1.** react

     b. build something large such as a building, bridge, or sculpture

_____ **2.** construct

     c. a fairly large area of a state, country, and so on

_____ **3.** circumstances

     d. behave in a particular way because of what someone has done or said to you

Use the academic words from the exercise above to complete the sentences.

4. The tri-state _____ includes New York, New Jersey, and Connecticut.

5. My dogs always _____ to visitors by barking a lot.

6. Students can leave the classroom only under certain _____.

7. Rick plans to _____ a model of the museum from blocks.

Complete the sentences with your own ideas.

Example: The circumstances surrounding the burglary were very ___*mysterious*___.

8. When I have a problem, I react by _____.

9. The states in my region include _____.

10. If I could build anything I wanted, I would construct

_____.

REMEMBER Two vowels can work as a team to stand for one vowel sound. The vowel team *ea* can stand for the long vowel /ē/ as in *treat*. It can also stand for the short vowel /e/ as in *spread*. In a few words, *ea* stands for the long vowel /ā/ as in *steak*. Knowing these sound spellings can help you say and spell many words correctly.

Read the words in the box below quietly to yourself. Notice what sound the vowel team *ea* stands for in each word. Then sort the words according to their sound spellings. Write each word in the correct column in the chart.

~~wreath~~	dread	great	sheath	bread
break	thread	cheat	break-in	

/ē/ spelled *ea*	/e/ spelled *ea*	/ā/ spelled *ea*
wreath		

Identify what sound the vowel digraph *ea* stands for in each word below. Then use each word in a sentence of your own.

Example: instead *ea stands for /e/   I wore a scarf instead of a hat.*

1. seal _____

2. bleach _____

3. breakthrough _____

4. dream _____

5. feather _____

6. widespread _____

7. leaf _____

READING STRATEGY   CLASSIFY   *Use with textbook page 283.*

REMEMBER When you classify, you arrange words, ideas, objects, texts, or people into groups with common characteristics.

Read each paragraph. Then answer the questions that follow.

Luisa loved sports. She was always playing softball, hockey, or soccer. Her brother Luis loved cooking. His dad taught him to make fried eggs and oatmeal when he was five. By the time he was eight, he could bake a cake from scratch and make pie crusts. At age ten, he could make an asparagus soufflé. Luisa loved his spaghetti with meat sauce. He always made it for her before she played a big game. She called it Luis's Lucky Spaghetti.

1. What words in this passage have to do with sports?

_____

_____

2. What words in this passage have to do with food?

_____

_____

Ben's mom was in the army, so the family often moved from place to place. He was born in Ohio. The family lived in Germany when he was two. When he was six, they moved to Japan. One day, they went to a kite festival, and Ben fell in love with kites. When they moved to Florida, he flew a flat kite on the beach. In Kansas, he learned to fly a box kite. Then, when they moved to Hawaii, he learned how to fly a sports kite.

3. What words in this passage have to do with different types of kites?

_____

4. What words in this passage have to do with places?

_____

5. How do you think classifying can make you a better reader?

_____

_____

Use with textbook page 288.

Choose the best answer for each item. Circle the letter of the correct answer.

1. Kids' Guernica is an international _____.

    a. school   **b.** peace project   **c.** movie

2. "Guernica" is a mural based on the _____.

    a. Spanish Civil War   **b.** American Revolutionary War   **c.** Vietnam War

3. "Guernica" was painted by _____.

    a. kids from all over   **b.** Yasuda Tadashi   **c.** Pablo Picasso

4. The artist painted "Guernica" to show the _____.

    a. importance of art   **b.** horror of war   **c.** thrill of winning

5. Kids' Guernica shows how everyday people _____.

    a. can make the world better   **b.** all like the same art   **c.** can all draw

EXTENSION *Use with textbook page 289.*

The chart below lists six places mentioned in the article. Write two facts about each place. The first one has been done for you.

Place	Fact	Fact
Japan	*has over 3,000 islands*	*capital is Tokyo*
Spain		
Israel		
France		
China		
Germany		

Name _____ Date _____

GRAMMAR, USAGE, AND MECHANICS

More Uses of the Present Perfect *Use with textbook page 290.*

REMEMBER Use the present perfect to talk about the past. The present perfect can describe an action that happened at an indefinite time in the past.
Example: Throughout history people *have fought* wars.
The present perfect can also describe events that started in the past and continue in the present.
Example: I *have lived* in Los Angeles for the past twenty years (and I am still living there now).
The present perfect is also often used to ask questions with the word *ever* and the corresponding answers with the word *never*.
Example: *Have* you *ever been* to Hawaii? No, I'*ve never been* to Hawaii.

Underline the correct verb form to complete each sentence.

Example: I (<u>have never seen</u> / never saw) such a beautiful painting.

1. Art (always was / has always been) important to me.

2. When I was a child, I (liked / have liked) scribbling on my parents' living room wall.

3. We first (heard / have heard) about the Guernica project in 2005.

4. Since then, my family (followed / has followed) its progress.

5. I (have never heard / never heard) about a more important art project for children.

Complete each sentence. Decide whether you need to use the present perfect or simple past.

Example: In 2004, the Guernica project ___*created a mural for the United Nations*___
___*building.*___

6. Since 2004, _____

7. In the past, _____

8. When Picasso was a young man, _____

9. Ever since she was a young woman, _____

10. Yesterday, _____

Write a Paragraph That Classifies Something *Use with textbook page 291.*

This is the chart that Koji completed before writing his paragraph.

Paintings	Plates	Sculptures
most well-known two dimensional wide range of realistic and abstract styles	three dimensional paintings and sculptural designs images of people and birds	three dimensional made with wood, clay, metal, stone, or combination wide range of realistic and abstract subjects

Complete your own chart for a paragraph about three types of art that you enjoy.

UNIT 5

How are courage and imagination linked?

READING 3: From *Hoot*

VOCABULARY　**Literary Words**　*Use with textbook page 293.*

REMEMBER Humor is anything that makes people laugh or amuses them. Writers use words and images to create humor. Writers also use **colorful language** to amuse their readers. Idioms, hyperbole, and slang are all examples of colorful language. *The apple of my eye* is an idiom. *I could eat a cow!* is hyperbole. *Yo, dude!* is slang.

Label each sentence as *humor* or *colorful language*.

Literary Word	Example
humor	Did you see this headline? "Astronaut takes blame for gas in spacecraft."
1.	I heard the gossip straight from the horse's mouth.
2.	What's worse than finding a worm in your apple? Finding half a worm!
3.	She is as honest as the day is long.
4.	What is the laziest vegetable? A couch potato!
5.	Who let the cat out of the bag and spoiled the surprise?

Write a sentence that contains either humor or colorful language next to each line.

Literary Element	Sentence
colorful language	*Give me an honest answer and don't pull my leg!*
6. humor	
7. colorful language	
8. humor	
9. colorful language	
10. humor	

Read the paragraph below. Pay attention to the underlined academic words.

An automobile company wants to build a factory next to the oldest park in our town. Almost everyone thinks this is a terrible site for a factory. The image of children playing and families picnicking right next to a factory is not at all attractive. Several groups are planning to demonstrate against the automobile company next week. They hope the city will deny the company's request to build a factory in that location.

Write the academic words from the paragraph above next to their correct definitions.

Example: _____*site*_____ : a place where something is being built or will be built

1. _____ : protest or support something in public with a lot of other people

2. _____ : a picture that you can see through a camera, on television, or in a mirror; a picture that you have in your mind

3. _____ : say that something is not true

Use the academic words from the paragraph above to complete the sentences.

4. Luci got a haircut and was shocked at her new _____.

5. The protestors will _____ against a store in place of the park.

6. The Atlantic Ocean is a new _____ for energy windmills.

7. The children _____ that they climbed the tree, but Mom knows they did.

Complete the sentences with your own ideas.

Example: The children see their image *in the water* _____.

8. Here is one thing I can deny: _____.

9. Something I would like to demonstrate against is _____.

10. In my town, the best site to build a new athletic complex is

_____.

WORD STUDY Prefixes *mega-, tele-, re-* Use with textbook page 295.

REMEMBER A prefix is a word part added to the beginning of a word that changes the word's meaning. For example, the prefix *re-* means "again." When you add *re-* to *view*, the new word *review* means "to view again." Knowing the meanings of prefixes can help you figure out many unfamiliar words.

Look at the chart below. Add the prefixes *mega-, tele-,* or *re-* to each base word to create a new word. Write the new word and its meaning in the chart.

Prefix	Base Word	New Word	Definition
mega-	byte	*megabyte*	*a unit for measuring computer information equal to a million bytes*
1. *mega-*	watt		
2. *tele-*	graph		
3. *tele-*	phone		
4. *re-*	cycle		
5. *re-*	fuel		

Create a new word by adding the prefix *mega-, tele-,* or *re-* to each word below. Then write the definition next to the new word. Check a dictionary if necessary.

Example: generate _regenerate: to bring back to life_

6. unite _____

7. vitamin _____

8. commuter _____

9. consider _____

10. vision _____

> **REMEMBER** When you summarize fiction, you write a few sentences about what happens in the story. When you summarize nonfiction, you write a few sentences about the main ideas.

Read each paragraph. Then answer the questions that follow.

It was supposed to be a two-hour sailing trip off the Maine Coast. But a sudden storm had brewed up. The little sailboat crashed into some rocks on a deserted island. Ashley and Courtney had to climb onto the rocky shore as their boat sank. They shivered under spruce trees as cold rain pelted down on them. "The thing is," Courtney said, "I forgot to leave Mom a note to tell her what we were doing."

1. What happens in this story?

   _____

   _____

2. Summarize why the girls are in danger.

   _____

   _____

People in ancient Rome had a healthy diet. They ate a lot of vegetables, such as cabbage, cauliflower, and carrots. They also ate beans like chickpeas and lentils. They loved bread. If they were rich, they could enjoy meat and fish. One of their flavorings was a sauce called *garum*. It was made of rotten fish. They used it on everything

3. What is the main idea of this text?

   _____

   _____

4. Summarize why the ancient Romans had a healthy diet.

   _____

   _____

5. How can the strategy of summarizing help you become a better reader?

   _____

   _____

Name _____ Date _____

COMPREHENSION   *Use with textbook page 304.*

Choose the best answer for each item. Circle the letter of the correct answer.

1. Roy and his friends are protesting against _____.

   a. owls   **b.** summer school   **c.** a new restaurant

2. Mullet Fingers claims the bucket is filled with _____.

   a. snapping turtles   **b.** bad poison   **c.** live cottonmouth
                                                                        snakes

3. The bucket is really filled with _____.

   a. huge spiders   **b.** toy snakes   **c.** angry bees

4. By the end of the story, Mother Paula is on the same side as _____.

   a. Chuck E. Muckle   **b.** the restaurant owners   **c.** Mullet Fingers

5. Chuck E. Muckle stands for _____.

   a. selfish, greedy people **b.** people who like pancakes   **c.** all rich people

RESPONSE to LITERATURE   *Use with textbook page 305.*

Imagine that you are Roy. How can you solve Mullet Fingers' problem? Write at least five lines.

_____

_____

_____

_____

_____

_____

_____

_____

_____

_____

_____

GRAMMAR, USAGE, AND MECHANICS

Quoted versus Reported Speech *Use with textbook page 306.*

REMEMBER Quoted speech reports the exact words someone else says. Quotation marks must be used to indicate the speaker's exact words.
Example: The teacher said, "It is time to read." The phrase announcing the quoted speech can stand before or after the speech.
Reported speech does not use the exact words when reporting what someone else says. The verb changes from present to past tense, and the word *that* is often added.
Example: The teacher said that it was time to read.

Underline the quoted speech and circle reported speech in the sentences.

Example: My mother always said, "Don't be late for school."

1. I heard him say that he liked my cooking.

2. The tourist said, "I really like this hotel."

For each sentence, rewrite quoted speech as reported speech and reported speech as quoted speech.

Example: "I am cold," she said.

   She said (that) she was cold.

3. The reporter announced, "All these young people want to save the wildlife."

   _____

4. But others yelled, "They are too late to save them."

   _____

5. They stated that these burrows had been abandoned for years.

   _____

WRITING AN EXPOSITORY PARAGRAPH

Write a Plot Summary *Use with textbook page 307.*

This is the plot summary chart that Brandon completed before writing his paragraph.

Main characters and setting:
Roy, Beatrice, and Mullet Fingers
Coconut Grove, FL

Characters' goals:
Stop a restaurant chain from building on land that is home to burrowing owls

Main events:
1. *Roy tries to stop the builders by speaking out.*
2. *Roy tries to convince the crowd by showing photos of the owls.*
3. *Mullet Fingers and Roy play a prank on Mr. Muckle.*

Outcome:
The main characters save the burrowing owls.

Complete your own plot summary chart for a paragraph that summarizes the plot of a story, novel, movie, or television show.

Main characters and setting:

Characters' goals:

Main events:

1.

2.

3.

Outcome:

How are courage and imagination linked?

READING 4: "A Tree Grows in Kenya: The Story of Wangari Maathai" / "How to Plant a Tree"

VOCABULARY **Key Words** *Use with textbook page 309.*

Write each word in the box next to its definition.

campaign	committee	continent	democratic	natural	nutrition

Example: ___*campaign*___ : a series of public actions to achieve a particular result

1. _____ : the process of getting the right food for good health and growth

2. _____ : one of the main areas of land on the earth

3. _____ : coming from nature; not made by people

4. _____ : a group of people chosen to do a particular job or make decisions

5. _____ : a system in which everyone has the same right to vote and speak

Use the words in the box at the top of the page to complete the sentences.

6. We had five steps in our _____ to elect Lee.

7. Vegetables are a good source of _____ to help you stay healthy.

8. Wool is a _____ fiber, not one made by people.

9. In a _____ government, the rule is "one vote, one person."

10. Asia is the largest _____, and Australia is the smallest one.

VOCABULARY   Academic Words   *Use with textbook page 310.*

Read the paragraph below. Pay attention to the underlined academic words.

Modern medical <u>technology</u> keeps advancing. Companies continue to develop new machines and devices that help cure diseases and <u>sustain</u> life. Every available <u>resource</u> is needed to develop these products. Private businesses and investors usually <u>finance</u> the new inventions. Governments, concerned about the <u>welfare</u> of people who will use them, usually check each <u>aspect</u> of the technology before they approve the new devices.

Write the letter of the correct definition next to each word.

Example: __*f*__ welfare

_____ **1.** technology

_____ **2.** resource

_____ **3.** aspect

_____ **4.** finance

_____ **5.** sustain

a. one of the parts or features of a situation, idea, or problem

b. something such as land, minerals, or natural energy that exists in a country and can be used in order to increase its wealth

c. make it possible for someone or something to continue to exist over time

d. provide money for something

e. a combination of all the knowledge, equipment, or methods used in scientific or industrial work

f. health, comfort, and happiness

Use the academic words from the exercise above to complete the sentences.

6. People need food and water to _____ life.

7. Gold is a valuable natural _____.

8. The class talked about one _____ of the book.

Complete the sentences with your own ideas.

Example: You should study finance so you can ___*manage your money*___.

9. My favorite technology is _____.

10. I sustain my good health by _____.

REMEMBER A *suffix* is a letter or letters added to the end of a word to make a new word. Suffixes can change a word's part of speech and meaning. If a base word ends in *e*, you usually drop the *e* when the suffix is added, as in *trombone* + *-ist* = *trombonist*, "one who plays the trombone."

Look at the chart below. Add the suffix *-ic, -ist,* or *-able* to create a new word. Write the new word in the chart. Then write the word's meaning and part of speech.

Word	Suffix	New Word	Meaning	Part of Speech
angel	*-ic*	*angelic*	*like an angel*	*adjective*
1. hero	*-ic*			
2. motor	*-ist*			
3. novel	*-ist*			
4. train	*-able*			
5. obtain	*-able*			

Create a new word by adding the suffix *-ic, -ist,* or *-able* to each word below. Then write the definition next to the new word. Check a dictionary if necessary.

Example: debate ___*+ able = debatable: able to be debated*___

  6. guitar _____

  7. wash _____

  8. idiot _____

  9. ideal _____

10. explain _____

READING STRATEGY | FOLLOW STEPS IN A PROCESS

Use with textbook page 311.

> **REMEMBER** When you follow steps in a process, you read the instructions about how to do something. Usually, the steps are arranged in chronological, or time, order, from first to last.

Read the paragraph below. Then answer the questions that follow.

Making bread isn't easy, but you can do it if you follow the recipe. First, you mix the yeast with sugar and warm water and let it sit for a little while. Then you mix dry ingredients. After that you mix the wet ingredients. Then you mix them together. Next, put the lump of dough on a surface covered with flour and knead them with your hands for ten minutes. Put the dough in a bowl and let it rise for about an hour. Punch it down, then make it into loaves. Let it rise again. Then bake it.

1. What is the first step in making bread?

   _____

   _____

2. What is the last step before putting the bread in the oven?

   _____

   _____

3. What are some of the words in the passage that show a new step will follow?

   _____

   _____

4. What conclusions can you make about baking bread from reading these steps?

   _____

   _____

5. How can following steps in a process help you to become a better reader?

   _____

   _____

Choose the best answer for each item. Circle the letter of the correct answer.

1. Wangari Maathai won the Nobel Prize for _____.

   a. working toward peace   **b.** art and music   **c.** being an excellent student

2. Maathai started an organization called _____.

   a. Kenyan Women   **b.** the Green Belt Movement   **c.** A Single Step

3. Some people in Kenya didn't like Maathai's ideas because she _____.

   a. always worked alone   **b.** didn't finish school   **c.** changed the way things are done

4. Maathai's main goal is to give people _____.

   a. a lot of money   **b.** awards   **c.** a better life

5. The first step in planting a tree is to _____.

   a. choose a good place   **b.** put the tree in the hole   **c.** water your tree

EXTENSION *Use with textbook page 317.*

Write five ways that Wangari Maathai helped the world and people in the chart. Then write ways that you can help the world and people. The first answer has been done for you.

How Maathai Helped the World	How I Can Help the World
She convinced people to plant trees.	*I can plant some trees in my town.*

GRAMMAR, USAGE, AND MECHANICS

Imperatives *Use with textbook page 318.*

> **REMEMBER** Imperatives request that an action is performed. Imperatives are used to give instructions, directions, or orders, and to make suggestions or requests. The subject of an imperative sentence is rarely mentioned. It is generally understood that a *you* is addressed by the imperative.
> **Example:** Don't drive too fast.
> Imperatives are most commonly used in instruction booklets or other how-to writing.

Mark each imperative with a ✓.

Example: ___✓___ Don't go out after dark!

_____ I don't think you should go out after dark.

1. _____ Can you help me?

_____ Help me!

2. _____ Turn off the light when you leave the room.

_____ Would you mind turning off the light when leaving the room?

3. _____ It is best to turn right at the intersection.

_____ Turn right at the intersection.

Rewrite each of the following sentences as an imperative. The first sentence has been done for you.

Example: You will be home on time.

   Be home on time. _____

4. You will read every day.

_____

5. You must work hard.

_____

WRITING AN EXPOSITORY PARAGRAPH

Write How-to Instructions *Use with textbook page 319.*

This is the steps-in-a-process chart that Danielle completed before writing her paragraph.

Water the tree where the roots are located.

↓

Widen the watering area as the tree grows.

↓

Place mulch around the tree.

↓

Don't fertilize the tree unless it is lacking in nutrients.

↓

Keep checking the tree.

Complete your own steps-in-a-process chart for a paragraph that gives instructions on how to do something.

↓

↓

↓

↓

EDIT AND PROOFREAD   *Use with textbook page 326.*

Read the paragraph carefully. Look for mistakes in spelling, punctuation, and grammar. Mark the mistakes with proofreader's marks (textbook page 454). Then rewrite the paragraph correctly on the lines.

Have you ever visited Puerto Rico? It is a group of ilands in the
caribbean. I was born in San Juan, Puerto Rico and lived their until
I was twelf years old. My mother says that Puerto rico is the most
byoutiful place on earth The island is filled with bloming flours. Many
afternoons, I sat beneeth a tree to smell the sweet hibiscus. Puerto Rico
is part of America. The United States president is our president, too.
Most people speak Spanish, many Puerto Ricans also speak English.
many people visit Puerto Rico every year for a vacation. Come for a visit
soon. it is warm and sunny all year!

_____

_____

_____

_____

_____

_____

_____

_____

_____

_____

Underline the vocabulary items you know and can use well. Review and practice any you haven't underlined. Underline them when you know them well.

Literary Words	Key Words	Academic Words	
setting the scene	anniversary	approach	aspect
list of characters	atomic bomb	convey	finance
stage directions	canvases	cooperate	resource
humor	chaos	drama	sustain
colorful language	inspiration	circumstances	technology
	mural	construct	welfare
	campaign	react	
	committee	region	
	continent	demonstrate	
	democratic	deny	
	natural	image	
	nutrition	site	

Put a check by the skills you can perform well. Review and practice any you haven't checked off. Check them off when you can perform them well.

Skills	I can . . .
Word Study	☐ spell words with *oo*. ☐ spell words with *ea*. ☐ recognize and use the prefixes *mega-*, *tele-*, and *re-*. ☐ recognize and use the suffixes *-ic*, *-ist*, and *-able*.
Reading Strategies	☐ analyze text structure. ☐ classify. ☐ summarize. ☐ follow steps in a process.
Grammar, Usage, and Mechanics	☐ use adverbs with *-ly*. ☐ use present perfect correctly. ☐ use quoted versus reported speech correctly. ☐ use imperatives.
Writing	☐ write a formal e-mail. ☐ write a paragraph that classifies something. ☐ write a plot summary. ☐ write how-to instructions. ☐ write an expository essay.

Name _____ Date _____

Learn about Art with the Smithsonian
American Art Museum *Use with textbook pages 328–329.*

LEARNING TO LOOK

Look at *The Throne of the Third Heaven of the Nations' Millennium General Assembly* by
James Hampton on page 329 in your textbook. Link to the Smithsonian American
Art Museum web site feature http://americanart.si.edu/collections/interact/zoom/
hampton_throne.cfm. Zoom in on Hampton's throne in more detail. Focus on one
section of the artwork. List as many details as possible about that one section.

Example: ___*There is a silver frame on the wall.*_____

1. _____

2. _____

3. _____

4. _____

5. _____

INTERPRETATION

Look at *The Throne of the Third Heaven of the Nations' Millennium General Assembly*
again. Imagine that you could create a work of art out of everyday objects like
Hampton did. List the objects you would use.

Example: ___*light bulb*_____

6. _____

7. _____

8. _____

9. _____

10. _____

Where would you display it? Why?

_____

_____

Look at *The Throne of the Third Heaven of the Nations' Millennium General Assembly* by James Hampton again. If you could interview James Hampton about this work of art, what would you ask him? Use *Who, What, Why, Where, When,* and *How* to frame your questions.

Example: Where ___*did you find all of the objects that you used?*___

11. Who _____

_____

12. Where _____

_____

13. When _____

_____

14. What _____

_____

15. Why _____

_____

16. How _____

_____

Name _____ Date _____

What is your vision of life in the future?

READING 1: *"Life in the Future"*

VOCABULARY **Key Words** *Use with textbook page 333.*

Write each word in the box next to its definition.

| artificial | canyons | frontier | mass-produced | ~~robots~~ | volcanoes |

Example: _____robots_____: machines that move and can do some of the work of humans.

1. _____: the area beyond the places people know well

2. _____: mountains with a large hole on top out of which lava, rock, and ashes sometimes explode

3. _____: not real or natural, but made by people

4. _____: produced in large numbers using machinery so that each object is the same and can be sold cheaply

5. _____: deep valleys with very steep sides

Use the words in the box at the top of the page to complete the sentences.

6. _____ that erupt underwater can cause huge waves.

7. Many _____ do work that is too dangerous for humans.

8. The _____ flowers look real!

9. The Southwest has many deep _____, but the Midwest is very flat.

10. Some people say that the sea is the last unexplored _____.

Read the paragraph below. Pay attention to the underlined academic words.

"Green" is the new <u>trend</u> in home design. The <u>occupation</u> of a green architect is to <u>research</u> what building materials and technology will be least harmful to the environment. Solar panels are a popular part of green design because their <u>function</u> is to use the natural rays of sunlight to power a home. Using natural energy and environmentally friendly materials is good for the planet and also usually saves money.

Write the academic words from the paragraph above next to their correct definitions.

Example: ___*function*___ : the usual purpose of a thing, or the job that someone usually does

1. _____ : job or profession

2. _____ : serious study of a subject that is intended to discover new facts about it

3. _____ : the way a situation is generally developing or changing

Use the academic words from the paragraph above to complete the sentences.

4. The scientist does _____ on diseases to try to find cures for them.

5. The latest fashion _____ for women is flat shoes.

6. The _____ of a fuse is to control electricity in a home.

7. Her _____ is teaching at the high school.

Complete the sentences with your own ideas.

Example: I have noticed a trend __*toward early retirement and part-time jobs*__ .

8. I want to do research on _____ .

9. The function of a car is to _____ .

10. The occupation I want when I grow up is _____ .

WORD STUDY Spelling the Diphthongs /oi/ and /ou/

Use with textbook page 335.

REMEMBER Some English words contain two vowel sounds that are said quickly so that the sounds glide into one another. The two sounds form a vowel sound called a diphthong. **Example:** *boil*

Look at the words in the word box. Write each word in the chart below under the column it belongs in and circle the diphthong in each word.

foil	mouse	brow	soy	proud	choice
voyage	broil	sound	frown	allow	employ

/oi/ as in *coin*	/oi/ as in *boy*	/ou/ as in *ground*	/ou/ as in *how*
f(oi)l			

Write two sentences with words that contain the /oi/ sound spelled *oi* or *oy* as indicated in parentheses.

1. (*oi*) _____

2. (*oy*) _____

Write two sentences with words that contain the /ou/ sound spelled *ou* or *ow* as indicated in parentheses.

3. (*ou*) _____

4. (*ow*) _____

> **REMEMBER** When you read, take notes. Keep track of the main idea and the details.

Read each paragraph. Then answer the questions that follow.

China is an ancient civilization that has contributed a great deal to the world. Thousands of years ago, the Chinese invented paper, the compass, gunpowder and printing. It is difficult to imagine life today without these inventions.

1. What is the main idea of the passage above?

_____

_____

2. What are the details in the passage above?

_____

_____

India is the largest democracy in the world. It is the second most highly populated country in the world after China. In terms of land mass, it is the seventh largest country on Earth.

3. What is the main idea of the passage above?

_____

_____

4. What are the details in the passage above?

_____

_____

5. How can the strategy of taking notes help you to understand what you read more clearly?

_____

_____

Name _____ Date _____

Choose the best answer for each item. Circle the letter of the correct answer.

1. Today, the world's population is _____.

   a. growing fast   **b.** shrinking fast   **c.** staying the same

2. A hypersonic plane will most likely _____.

   a. fly slowly   **b.** fly very fast   **c.** cost very little

3. Jetpacks will let people _____.

   a. fly without planes   **b.** stay healthy   **c.** be in movies

4. The authors think the future will most likely have many _____.

   a. creatures from outer space   **b.** rich people   **c.** wonderful inventions

5. The authors imagine the future as _____.

   a. different from today   **b.** worse than today   **c.** the same as today

EXTENSION   *Use with textbook page 343.*

This article tells about the future. In the left column, write what the article thinks will happen in the future. In the right column, write what you think will happen. The first one is done for you.

What the Article Thinks about the Future	What I Think about the Future
Robots: *Some countries will have more robots than people*	*Robots will never become popular.*
Cities:	
Cars:	
Planes:	
Jetpacks:	
Living on Other Planets:	

Different Ways of Expressing Predictions *Use with textbook page 344.*

> **REMEMBER** There are several ways to predict what the future may bring. Use *will* plus the base form of a verb to talk about things you are certain will happen in the future.
> **Example:** The new president will take office in January.
> If you are not certain that an event will happen, you can use *may/could* plus the base form of a verb.
> **Example:** I may celebrate my birthday in Hawaii this year.
> You can also use *probably/maybe/perhaps* plus *will* and the base form of a verb to talk about things you are not certain will happen.
> **Example:** Perhaps I will spend the summer at home this year.

Underline the sentence if the speaker is certain about the predictions. Circle the sentence if the speaker is not certain about the predictions.

Example: <u>Future cars will be more fuel-efficient.</u>

1. Perhaps space travel will be the vacation of the future.

2. In the years to come, people may never leave their apartment buildings.

Circle the correct underlined word to complete each sentence.

Example: Fifty years from now, robots will <u>maybe</u> / (<u>probably</u>) do the housework.

3. In the week before exams, people <u>may / perhaps</u> be studying hard.

4. When I am old enough to marry and have children, there <u>probably / could</u> be flying cars.

5. I <u>perhaps / will</u> go to Europe sometime in the future.

WRITING A RESEARCH REPORT

Write an Introductory Paragraph *Use with textbook page 345.*

This is the inverted pyramid that Anna completed to narrow her topic.

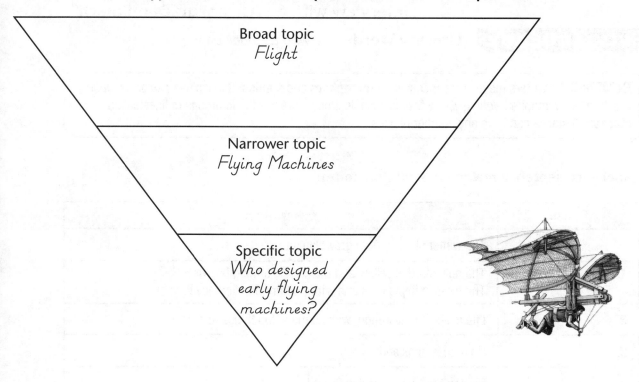

Broad topic
Flight

Narrower topic
Flying Machines

Specific topic
Who designed early flying machines?

Complete your own inverted pyramid to narrow a topic related to life in the future.

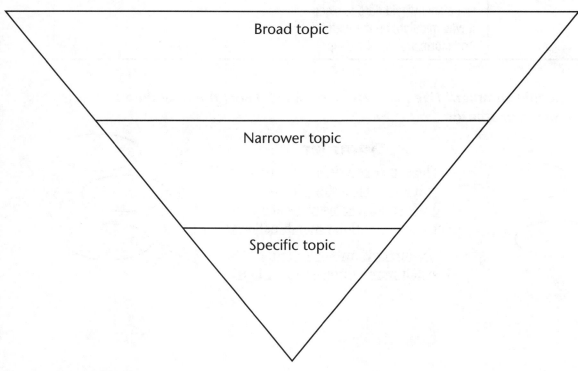

Broad topic

Narrower topic

Specific topic

UNIT 6

What is your vision of life in the future?

READING 2: "Southbound on the Freeway" /
"Cardinal Ideograms" /
"Interview with an Astronaut: Dan Bursch"

VOCABULARY Literary Words *Use with textbook page 347.*

REMEMBER Writers make comparisons with **metaphors** and **similes**. Similes use *like* or *as*. *John is a bear* is a metaphor. *John is like a bear* is a simile. Poems are written in groups of lines called **stanzas**. A stanza can have any number of lines.

Label each sentence *metaphor, simile,* **or** *stanza.*

Sense	Description
metaphor	The winter sky is a dirty grey blanket.
1.	The goldenrod is yellow and the corn is turning brown, The trees in apple orchards with fruit are bending down.
2.	Life is like a playground, with so many fun things to do!
3.	No man is an island.
4.	Playing the trumpet is like flying in the sky.
5.	We were crowded in the cabin, Not a soul would dare to sleep— It was midnight on the waters, And storm was on the deep.

Read the poem "Summer." Five parts are underlined. Label the underlined parts as *metaphor, simile,* **or** *stanza.*

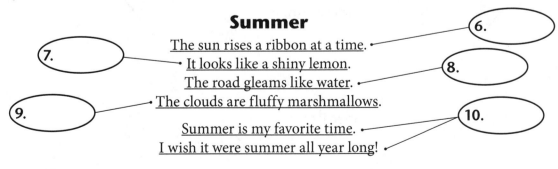

Summer

6.

7. The sun rises a ribbon at a time.
It looks like a shiny lemon.
8. The road gleams like water.
9. The clouds are fluffy marshmallows.

10. Summer is my favorite time.
I wish it were summer all year long!

VOCABULARY **Academic Words** *Use with textbook page 348.*

Read the paragraph below. Pay attention to the underlined academic words.

> Our book club meets once a month in the lounge <u>section</u> of our public library. We mostly read books that have been <u>published</u> recently. Sometimes the books concern fairly simple themes, and sometimes they are more <u>complex</u>. One of my favorite parts of the meetings is when everyone shares their <u>interpretation</u> of the book.

Write the letter of the correct definition next to each word.

Example: ___*c*___ section   **a.** complicated

_____ **1.** published   **b.** an explanation

_____ **2.** complex   **c.** a part of something

_____ **3.** interpretation   **d.** printed and sold

Use the academic words from the exercise above to complete the sentences.

4. We live in the northern _____ of town.

5. The directions were so _____ that no one understood them!

6. My sister's _____ of the cave painting is the same as mine.

7. Cesar _____ a story about his life in America.

Complete the sentences with your own ideas.

Example: A race car is complex, *because there are many parts that run together* .

8. My interpretation of paintings is based on _____.

9. The club published a schedule of its _____.

10. My favorite section of the newspaper is _____.

REMEMBER Many English words come from Greek and Latin word parts called roots. Knowing the meaning of a Greek or Latin root can help you figure out the meaning of a new word.
Example: The prefix *uni-* means one. A *uniform* means *one particular type of clothing worn by all members of a group.*

Review the prefixes and roots in the chart.

Prefixes		Roots	
uni- ("one")	tri- ("three")	cycle ("round")	verse ("turn")
bi- ("two")	re- ("again")	spec ("see")	

Look at the words below. In each word, underline any prefixes or roots from the chart above. Think about how the prefix or root helps you understand the meaning. Then write a definition of each word. Use a dictionary if needed.

Example: <u>uni</u>te *to bring together*

 1. triangle _____

 2. spectator _____

 3. recycle _____

 4. unique _____

 5. trilogy _____

 6. reverse _____

 7. billion _____

 8. spectacular _____

 9. bilingual _____

10. biweekly _____

Write sentences using one of the words you defined in the exercise above.

11. _____

12. _____

13. _____

READING STRATEGY ANALYZE TEXT STRUCTURE 2

Use with textbook page 349.

> **REMEMBER** When you read, analyze text structure by noticing how the text is presented. A poem is presented in stanzas. A script contains the names of characters in all caps, followed by a colon. After the colon, the character's lines of dialogue are presented.

Read each passage and answer the questions that follow.

> Rose petals are red
> Bluebirds are blue
> Everything we said
> Is perfectly true

1. What is the text structure of the passage above? How do you know?

_____

> JAMES: Where is the party?
> JOHN: What party?
> JAMES: The party that Alex and Sonia are throwing.
> JOHN: I didn't even know they were throwing a party!

2. What is the text structure of the passage above? How do you know?

_____

3. What do the names in all capital letters represent?

_____

4. What does text after a colon represent in the passage above?

_____

5. How can the strategy of analyzing text structure help you to understand what you read?

_____

Choose the best answer for each item. Circle the letter of the correct answer.

1. The tourist in "Southbound on the Freeway" decides that people on Earth are _____.

   a. measuring tapes   **b.** cars   **c.** worms

2. The poem "Cardinal Ideograms" describes _____.

   a. numbers   **b.** people from outer space   **c.** birds

3. Astronaut Dan Bursch finds being in space _____.

   a. boring   **b.** just like being on Earth   **c.** interesting

4. The tourist in "Southbound on the Freeway" and the speaker in "Cardinal Ideograms" look at common things _____.

   a. in the same way   **b.** in new ways   **c.** from outer space

5. The two poems and the interview are the same because they all describe _____.

   a. seeing familiar things in a new way   **b.** life on another planet   **c.** flying around Earth

RESPONSE TO LITERATURE *Use with textbook page 359.*

Write a short poem about what you think Earth will be like in 100 years. Try to use information from the two poems and the interview.

_____

_____

_____

_____

_____

_____

_____

_____

_____

GRAMMAR, USAGE, AND MECHANICS

Different Ways of Asking Questions *Use with textbook page 360.*

REMEMBER Questions can be asked with the 5Ws: *Who? What? When? Where? Why?* You can also ask *How?* and *yes/no* questions. There are certain phrases that help you ask questions such as *I would like to know* or *I want to ask.*

Complete each sentence. Choose a word or phrase from the chart.

Where	I would like to know	~~How many times~~	Why

Example: _How many times_ have you traveled to the moon already?

1. _____ does mankind want to explore space?

2. _____ do you want to go next?

3. _____ what kind of work you do at the space station.

Rewrite each sentence into a question about the underlined part of the sentence.

Example: Neil Armstrong walked on the moon <u>in 1969</u>.

When did Neil Armstrong walk on the moon?

4. <u>Twelve people</u> have walked on the moon.

_____

5. We share the work <u>because there is so much to be done</u>.

_____

Write five questions you'd like to ask an astronaut.

6. _____

7. _____

8. _____

9. _____

10. _____

Support a Main Idea with Examples *Use with textbook page 361.*

This is the main idea/examples web that Koji completed before writing his paragraph.

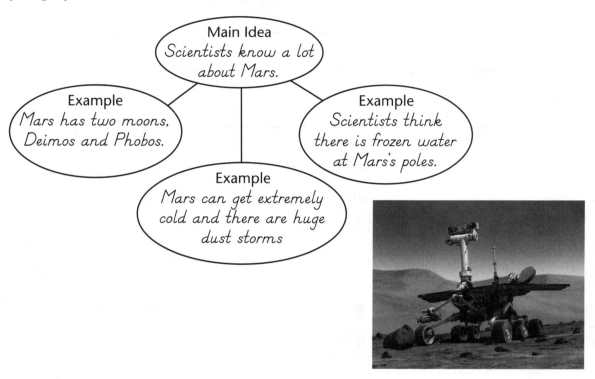

Complete your own main idea/examples web for a paragraph about space missions or astronauts.

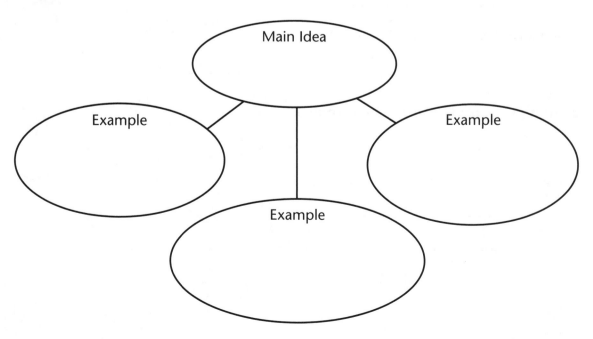

Name _____   Date _____

UNIT 6

What is your vision of life in the future?

READING 3: From *The Time Warp Trio: 2095*

VOCABULARY **Literary Words** *Use with textbook page 363.*

> **REMEMBER** **Science fiction** is writing that imagines what life will be like in the future. It often uses ideas from science and technology. **Setting** is the time and place where an event or story takes place. The setting can be real or make believe. Writers can tell you about the setting or give you clues in the story to figure it out.

Label each passage as *science fiction* or *setting*.

Literary Word	Example
setting	On a rainy November morning in 1776, a soldier walked up the dusty path in Virginia.
1.	It was a week before the Lhari ship went into warp drive, so Greg was bored. He felt glad when he saw the Juak medic coming to prepare him for cold-sleep.
2.	It is after dinner in January 1906, in the living room of Dr. Smith's house in London.
3.	It is 2007, in a small apartment in the back of a building in St. Louis.
4.	The creature had 16 arms and legs. It was green and slimy. It spoke in a creepy, high voice.
5.	Kea was going home to Pluto from school on Venus. "I'm glad the trip takes only an hour," she said as she put on her space suit.

Read the passage "Rebels of the Red Planet." Underline the words that show setting and circle words that imagine what life will be like in the future. The first example is done for you.

> ## Rebels of the Red Planet
>
> It was 5:00 P.M. The car bumped on the rocky road on Mars. The desert stretched to the distant horizon. It was silent and empty. The steel-blue sky shimmered above the red surface. The zeuzes made their odd noises as they flew backwards in the sky. The rebels adjusted their space suits, helmets, and oxygen tanks. Dark Kensington, more than 500 years old, decided that today he would overthrow the evil ruler who gripped the settlers on Mars.

Read the paragraph below. Pay attention to the underlined academic words.

> The goal of a persuasive speech is to <u>shift</u> the opinion of the listener. Successful speakers use a number of <u>strategies</u> to get and hold the attention of the listener. Common <u>techniques</u> include using catchy phrases, expressive body language, and the use of visuals. Good speeches also need to include a number of <u>specific</u> details about the subject, so that the listener believes the speaker is an expert.

Write the academic words from the paragraph above next to their correct definitions.

Example: _____*shift*_____: a change in the way most people think about something, or in the way something is done

1. _____: special methods of doing something

2. _____: sets of plans and skills used in order to gain success or achieve an aim

3. _____: detailed and exact

Use the academic words from the paragraph above to complete the sentences.

4. Her _____ for getting to school on time are simple.

5. The teacher asked _____ questions about the characters in the novel.

6. The artist uses the _____ of dry brush and shading in her paintings.

7. I hope my school will _____ its policy on lateness.

Complete the sentences with your own ideas.

Example: The athlete's strategies for winning include
*getting a lot of sleep and drinking lots of water*.

8. I wish our library would shift its rules about _____.

9. When my family travels, we usually have specific questions about

_____.

10. I think techniques for building future cities will include

_____.

Name _____ Date _____

WORD STUDY **Schwa spelled *a, e, i, o, u*** *Use with textbook page 365.*

REMEMBER The "uh" sound in a word is called a schwa. The symbol for the schwa is the letter *e* turned upside down. In multisyllabic words, the schwa occurs only in an unstressed syllable.
Example: In the word *lesson*, the schwa is in the second syllable.

Look at the words below. Say each word out loud. Circle the syllable that is stressed. Then, underline the schwa in each word.

pencil	about	cotton	confront	away
hurtful	sister	supply	utensil	broken

Write each word in the word box above in the chart below. Place each word under its correct column. Use a dictionary if needed.

Schwa spelled *e*	Schwa spelled *i*	Schwa spelled *o*	Schwa spelled *a*	Schwa spelled *u*

Write ten new words that have the schwa sound in an unstressed syllable. Circle the schwa. Use a dictionary if needed.

1. _____   6. _____

2. _____   7. _____

3. _____   8. _____

4. _____   9. _____

5. _____   10. _____

> **REMEMBER** Before you read, skim the text to get a sense of what it is about. When you skim, you read the text quickly. Glance at the title, text and illustrations. Make predictiions about what you think the selection will be about.

Use the text to answer the questions that follow.

Homes of the Future

What will homes of the future look like? Will they even be on planet Earth or on another planet? Writers and artists love to imagine cities and homes of the future. Science fiction writers especially enjoy picturing homes of the future. Sometimes they envision houses that look like space ships. Other times, they imagine homes that are underwater or deep underground. New materials may make it possible to build extremely large homes very cheaply. It may be possible to live in a home that is woven from super strong carbon threads! One thing is for sure: if the homes of the future are anything like the way writers and artists picture them, life in the future is going to be very interesting.

1. Circle the title. What can you guess the article will be about from reading the title?

   _____

2. Circle the illustration. What does the illustration tell you about the content of the article?

   _____

3. Skim the text. What is the main idea of the text?

   _____

4. Predict what the text will be about.

   _____

5. How can the strategy of skimming help you to become an active reader?

   _____

Name _____ Date _____

Choose the best answer for each item. Circle the letter of the correct answer.

1. This story takes place in _____.

   a. New York City   **b.** Florida   **c.** South America

2. *The Book* is important because it is _____.

   a. a medical record   **b.** filled with money   **c.** a time-travel guide

3. The three boys and the three girls look alike because they _____.

   a. wear the same clothing   **b.** are the same age   **c.** are related to each other

4. This story is _____.

   a. serious   **b.** funny   **c.** scary

5. This story is science fiction because the characters _____.

   a. can travel through time   **b.** have a good time   **c.** are all very smart

RESPONSE TO LITERATURE *Use with textbook page 373.*

Imagine that you are Sam, Fred, and Joe. What can you do to solve your problem? Write at least five lines.

_____

_____

_____

_____

_____

_____

Using Punctuation *Use with textbook page 374.*

REMEMBER Punctuation helps readers understand what you want to say. Use a period at the end of a statement. Use a question mark at the end of a question. Use an exclamation point at the end of a sentence expressing strong feelings. Commas are used to separate words in a series, introductory words or phrases, and quotations.
Examples: She bought shirts, pants, and shoes. After breakfast, he went jogging. He asked, "Where is the ticket?"

Place a ✓ next to the sentence with the correct punctuation.

1. _____ Don't worry, I'd be glad to help you?

   _____ Don't worry. I'd be glad to help you.

2. _____ "Excuse me," she asked. "What time does the movie start?"

   _____ "Excuse me." She asked, "what time does the movie start."

3. _____ I can't make heads or tails of this, Please help me.

   _____ I can't make heads or tails of this. Please help me!

4. _____ I was really worried about you. Where were you?

   _____ I was really worried about you? Where were you!

5. _____ When I went shopping I bought tomatoes, cucumbers, lettuce, and radishes.

   _____ When I went shopping I bought tomatoes, cucumbers lettuce and radishes!

Punctuate each sentence below.

6. What a wonderful surprise

7. If we want to catch the bus she said we really have to hurry

8. We've seen Paris Berlin London Rome and Vienna

9. Don't forget to bring your backpack

10. Can I help you with your homework assignment

11. Before I left home I made a sandwich

12. Are you sure she asked you want to go

13. The woman asked Do you want peas carrots or potatoes

WRITING A RESEARCH REPORT

Include Quotations and Citations *Use with textbook page 375.*

This is the main idea/details web that Andrew completed before writing his paragraph.

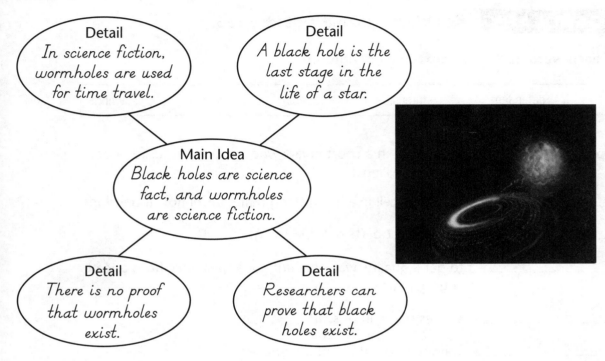

> **Detail**
> *In science fiction, wormholes are used for time travel.*

> **Detail**
> *A black hole is the last stage in the life of a star.*

> **Main Idea**
> *Black holes are science fact, and wormholes are science fiction.*

> **Detail**
> *There is no proof that wormholes exist.*

> **Detail**
> *Researchers can prove that black holes exist.*

Complete your own main idea/details web for a paragraph about time travel or science fiction.

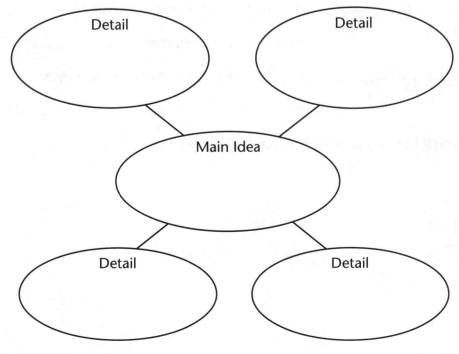

> **Detail**

> **Detail**

> **Main Idea**

> **Detail**

> **Detail**

What is your vision of life in the future?

READING 4: "Genetic Fingerprints"

VOCABULARY **Key Words** *Use with textbook page 377.*

Write each word in the box next to its definition.

cells	~~defendant~~	forensic	genes	inherit	whorls

Example: ___*defendant*___ : the person in a court of law who has been accused of doing something illegal

1. _____: parts of a cell in a living thing that control how it develops

2. _____: the smallest parts of living things

3. _____: to get a quality, way of acting, or appearance from one of your parents.

4. _____: shapes that curl or swirl

5. _____: ways to find out about a crime

Use the words in the box at the top of the page to complete the sentences.

6. _____ evidence can include hair, DNA, and fingerprints.

7. Children get _____ for many traits from their parents.

8. She hopes the baby will _____ her father's deep brown eyes.

9. The _____ said, "I am innocent of the crime!"

10. You can tell one set of fingerprints from another by its _____.

VOCABULARY   **Academic Words** *Use with textbook page 378.*

Read the paragraph below. Pay attention to the underlined academic words.

> Every underline{generation} is feeling the rising cost of medical care in the United States. Many are finding they can no longer afford health insurance. And for those who have insurance, there are often expensive extra charges for a medical procedure. Lawmakers are considering legislation to help make medical care more affordable. Some even feel that national healthcare, where the government pays for medical treatment, would be a good policy.

Write the letter of the correct definition next to each word.

Example: ___e___ procedure

_____ 1. generation

_____ 2. policy

_____ 3. legislation

_____ 4. medical

a. all the people who are about the same age, especially in a family

b. a law or set of laws

c. relating to medicine and the treatment of disease or injury

d. a way of doing things that has been officially agreed upon and chosen by a political party or organization

e. the correct or normal way of doing something

Use the academic words from the exercise above to complete the sentences.

5. The store has a return _____ posted on the wall.

6. Nurses and doctors are _____ experts.

7. The police use a specific _____ for taking your fingerprints.

Complete the sentences with your own ideas.

Example: People go to the medical center for __*treatment when they are sick*__.

8. Our government should pass legislation to _____.

9. Three people in my generation are _____.

10. The procedure for brushing your teeth is _____.

REMEMBER Many words in English have more than one meaning. When you read a sentence with one of these words, think about the context of the sentence to figure out which meaning fits. Also think about the part of speech of the word. Some words in English can be used as a verb as well as a noun.

Read each sentence. The boldfaced word in each sentence is a multiple-meaning word. In the space provided, write its part of speech and definition. Use a dictionary if needed.

1. There is a **bat** flying around the attic. _____

2. I cannot wait until it is my turn to **bat**. _____

3. I have found my mitt, but cannot find my **bat**. _____

4. Tonight I am going to the theater to see a **play**. _____

5. Do you **play** basketball? _____

6. Let us go outside and **play**. _____

7. I am going out for a **run**. _____

8. My mother is **running** for president. _____

9. I have to **train** before working as a waitress. _____

10. I caught the **train** just before it left the station. _____

The words *foot* and *roll* have multiple meanings. For each word, write sentences using different meanings of the word. Use a dictionary if needed

11. foot _____

12. foot _____

13. roll _____

14. roll _____

15. roll _____

READING STRATEGY | MAKE GENERALIZATIONS

Use with textbook page 379.

> **REMEMBER** When you read nonfiction, make generalizations about what you have read. A generalization is a statement or rule that applies to most examples and can be supported by facts.

Read the paragraph below and answer the questions that follow.

You may have heard the saying, *"An apple a day keeps the doctor away."* Well, it turns out to be true! Scientists have proven that eating apples on a daily basis can reduce your risk of developing many kinds of cancers. Moreover, apples are a great source of Vitamin C.

1. Does the passage above support the generalization: "Apples are good for your health"?

   _____

2. Explain your reasoning for the answer you gave to question number 1.

   _____

   _____

3. Does the passage above support the generalization: "Eating an apple a day will mean that you will never develop any form of cancer"?

   _____

4. Explain your reasoning for the answer you gave to question number 3.

   _____

   _____

5. How can the strategy of making generalizations help you to become a better reader?

   _____

   _____

Choose the best answer for each item. Circle the letter of the correct answer.

1. DNA is a _____.

   a. chemical set of   **b.** plant or animal   **c.** type of print
   instructions

2. Sir Alec Jeffreys discovered how to make a _____.

   a. DNA ladder   **b.** radioactive substance   **c.** genetic fingerprint

3. Now, DNA can be used to _____.

   a. write old books   **b.** fight bacteria   **c.** tell the future

4. Information gathered from DNA _____.

   a. is only used in   **b.** is cheap and easy   **c.** has many different uses
   court cases

5. DNA is so important because it _____.

   a. makes us who we are   **b.** is brand new   **c.** is very popular

EXTENSION   *Use with textbook page 385.*

Write five ways the article shows how DNA can be used now. Then explain why each way is important. An example is done for you.

How DNA Can Be Used Now	Why This is Important
to determine if a subject committed a crime	The right person can be punished for the crime.

GRAMMAR, USAGE, AND MECHANICS

Using Quotation Marks *Use with textbook page 386.*

REMEMBER Quotation marks are used to enclose a speaker's exact words or thoughts. This includes dialogue in a narrative.
Example: The little girl screamed in horror: "A spider! There's a spider on my ankle!"
In expository writing and research, quotation marks are used to signify a person's exact words, thoughts or writing.
Example: The scientist contradicted: "DNA tests have shown the opposite."
Quotation marks are also used to signify technical terms, unfamiliar slang, or unusual expressions.
Example: Our justice system prescribes that guilt must be proven beyond "reasonable doubt."
A word or phrase that defines another word can also be enclosed in quotation marks.
Example: DNA stands for "deoxyribonucleic acid."
Finally, enclose short book, article, or movie titles in quotation marks.
Example: "The Raven" by Edgar Allan Poe.

Mark an *X* next to each sentence that uses quotation marks correctly.

Example: _____ "He said:" Come to my house for dinner.

   ___*X*___ He said: "Come to my house for dinner."

1. _____ X-rays are also "called Röntgen rays."

   _____ X-rays are also called "Röntgen rays."

2. _____ "Please forgive me!" she pleaded.

   _____ Please forgive me, she pleaded.

3. _____ "You are a good friend," said Rita.

   _____ You are a good friend, "said Rita."

Add quotation marks to each sentence.

Example: "Can you help me find my mother?" the little boy asked.

4. Romeo is a character in Shakespeare's Romeo and Juliet.

5. Shakespeare's plays have been called the greatest plays in history.

Include Paraphrases and Citations *Use with textbook page 387.*

This is the main idea/details web that Angelina completed before writing her paragraph.

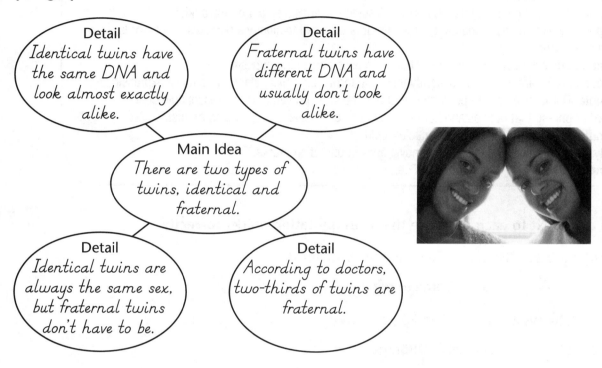

Detail
Identical twins have the same DNA and look almost exactly alike.

Detail
Fraternal twins have different DNA and usually don't look alike.

Main Idea
There are two types of twins, identical and fraternal.

Detail
Identical twins are always the same sex, but fraternal twins don't have to be.

Detail
According to doctors, two-thirds of twins are fraternal.

Complete your own main idea/details web for a paragraph about DNA.

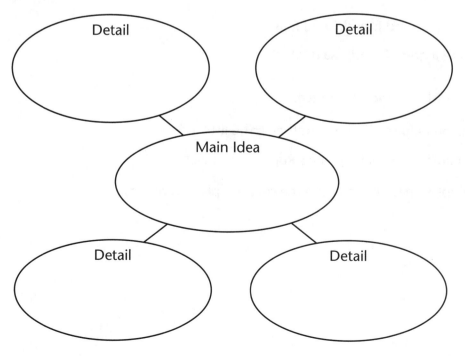

Detail

Detail

Main Idea

Detail

Detail

EDIT AND PROOFREAD   *Use with textbook page 396.*

Read the paragraph below carefully. Look for mistakes in spelling, punctuation, and grammar. Mark the mistakes with proofreader's marks (textbook page 454). Then rewrite the paragraph correctly on the lines below.

Anamals, like people, need exercise to stay healthy. Your pet will enjoy exercise a lot more if you do it safeley. Otherwise, your pet may get badly hurt. For example, last week I wos watching a man run on the bike path with his dog. The dog tripped the man and they both fell. I asked, Can I help you? I was glad they were not hurt. You hav to look aftur your anamals when you exeraze. Give your dog plenty of cool water before, during, and after all exeraze. Follow these rools to have fun and keep your pet healthy.

_____

_____

_____

_____

_____

_____

_____

_____

_____

_____

Use after completing page 397.

Underline the vocabulary items you know and can use well. Review and practice any you haven't underlined. Underline them when you know them well.

Literary Words	Key Words	Academic Words	
simile	artificial	function	generation
metaphor	canyons	occupation	legislation
stanzas	frontier	research	medical
science fiction	mass-produced	trend	policy
setting	robots	complex	procedure
	volcanoes	interpretation	
	cells	published	
	defendant	section	
	forensic	shift	
	genes	specific	
	inherit	strategies	
	whorls	techniques	

Put a check by the skills you can perform well. Review and practice any you haven't checked off. Check them off when you can perform them well.

Skills	I can . . .
Word Study	☐ recognize and spell diphthongs /oi/ and /ou/. ☐ recognize Greek and Latin roots. ☐ recognize and pronounce the schwa spelled a, e, i, o, u. ☐ identify and use multiple meaning words.
Reading Strategies	☐ take notes. ☐ analyze text structure. ☐ skim. ☐ make generalizations.
Grammar, Usage, and Mechanics	☐ use different ways of expressing predictions. ☐ use different ways of asking questions. ☐ use punctuation correctly. ☐ use quotation marks correctly.
Writing	☐ write an introductory paragraph. ☐ support a main idea with examples. ☐ include quotations and citations. ☐ include paraphrases and citations. ☐ write a research report.

Learn about Art with the Smithsonian
American Art Museum *Use with textbook pages 398–399.*

Look at *Sculpture Group Symbolizing World's Communication in the Atomic Age* by Harry Bertoia on page 399 in your textbook. **Describe six things you see in this artwork. State facts, not opinions.**

Example: _____ *star* _____

1. _____   4. _____

2. _____   5. _____

3. _____   6. _____

Look at *San Francisco to New York in One Hour* by Alexander Maldonado on page 398 in your textbook. **Imagine you are in this painting. Describe the scene.**

Example: _____ *I am in a car inside the tube. It is going very fast . . .* _____

What are you doing?

_____

_____

_____

_____

Where are you going?

_____

_____

_____

_____

5W&H

Look at *San Francisco to New York in One Hour* by Alexander Maldonado on page 398 in your textbook. Imagine you could interview the artist about his painting. What would you ask him? Use *Who, What, Why, Where, When* and *How* to frame your questions.

Example: Why _*did you choose this title for the painting?*_____

1. Who _____

_____

2. What _____

_____

3. Why _____

_____

4. Where _____

_____

5. When _____

_____

6. How _____

_____